THE GAME OF LIFE

Regine,
Thank you so much
for your love & support
& taking the time out to
Read my passion project.
I pray that my book blesses
you on this journey through
life. Keep believing that
for the impossible, He
is able. love you!
wait well,
Dacia

THE GAME
OF LIFE

Releasing The Weight When God Says Wait

DACIA JAMES LEWIS

WOMEN WIVES WARRIORS

Published by Women Wives Warriors. www.womenwiveswarriors.com
ISBN 978-1-7355076-0-6 (Paperback)
ISBN 978-1-7355076-1-3 (Hardcover)
ISBN 978-1-7355076-2-0 (eBook)

Cover design & photo: Louis Cuthbert

All the stories in this book are true, but names have been changed to protect the privacy of the people mentioned.

To My Husband, Walter.

You are the real MVP. I am not sure this book would exist if it were not for your gentle pushes—and coaching tactics. "How do you eat an elephant, Dacia? Huh? One piece at a time. Get Her Done!" Well, I'm done eating this elephant thanks to you. I love you.

To My Kids.

Look, you might not be here yet but once you arrive (and of age), read mama's book. Okay! Mostly because I said so. But also, because I wrote it as we waited for you. I hope it teaches you how to release all of your cares to the Most High God. And when seasons of waiting cause you to be frustrated or disappointed, I give you permission to have a temper tantrum. Cry, scream, shout—tell God exactly how you feel. Then wipe the tears, sit silently in His presence and if you don't hear a word from Him, relax. He's there. Never take His silence for absence. Choose to believe that no matter what you see, or don't see—His promises are true.

Don't give up; don't be impatient; be entwined as one with the Lord. Be brave and courageous, and never lose hope. Yes, keep on waiting—for He will never disappoint you!

Psalm 27:14 (TPT)

Contents

Contents

From Dacia

I empathize with those who are experiencing a waiting season.

To those who feel God has abandoned you and if you haven't one day you might:

My prayer is that God will penetrate your heart with His love, heal you of any infirmities, release you from the weight of all disappointments, and revive your faith in His promises. My hope is that His answers to me coupled with my experience through the waiting game will ignite a fire within you to believe God for the miraculous and wait in expectation. You are not forgotten in this season!

To those who carried or are carrying the same burden:

"If anybody feels you ... I feel you." May God help you find wisdom and peace in your journey and, more importantly, the courage to talk about your struggles and possibly help lift the weight from someone around you suffering from the devices that accompany undisclosed (or disclosed) *infertility*.

To ALL that are holding this book in their hands:

So that this book is NOT just a moment in history, but lives with you through your waiting seasons, I have included a 14-day devotional to help you wait in faith. Now, grab some popcorn, a blanket, a cup of hot cocoa or a glass of iced tea and prepare to laugh, smile, cry, pause, and repeat as I share some insane moments with you. If you need a recess from the weight of my story at any point, jump over to the Rules of Engagement section for some comic relief before you continue.

The Game of Life

Life is like a box of chocolates. You never know what you're going to get.

-Forrest Gump

As a kid, next to *Monopoly*, my favorite board game was LIFE. The idea of an excursion through adulthood made for quite an entertaining evening with friends. For hours, we explored the possibilities of life at the fate of a spinning wheel. The rules of the game require you to place your car on the board and insert a peg that represents navigating through life. One spin and you're off!

All of life's events jam-packed into one board game: college, career, marriage, buying a home, having kids, and retirement. Even unexpected hiccups make the way onto the board: job termination, mid-life crisis, stock market crashes, speeding tickets, and bill collectors. I'd say this game is pretty darn accurate! Wouldn't you?

The white picket fence and "The American Dream" seem easily attainable as life moves fictitiously fast on the board game. Marriage and even an "addition to the family" is possible. Luck inevitably lands you on a space that reads: baby boy, baby girl, or even twins. The possibilities were endless. It was as simple as landing on the square and adding a blue (baby boy) or pink (baby girl) peg into your automobile as you gallop on your venture through life with your pegged spouse by your side.

My friends and I enjoyed playing LIFE and since I only remember playing it with girls, I have concluded that adolescent boys just weren't interested in imitating such nonsense at a young age. But for me, I loved the game. In it, my life always seemed to go as planned and if not, I had options. I could either play until I redeemed the life I desired, or I could clear the board and start a new life.

If only our lives could be that simple. Given the option to choose the squares we want to land on, many of us might skip to *payday*, move ahead two spaces to a promotion, trade places with another player to jump over stress, leap over pain, or park in a burden-free square without hesitation. Real life is far from its traditional board game avatar. Just when you think everything is going according to plan, God interrupts your regularly scheduled program with an unpredictable bump in the road. And the *game* begins; welcome to the GAME OF LIFE.

Exposed

I believe that one of the most powerful ways we can share the Gospel with others is by connecting it with our own stories … and journey of faith.

-Ryan Stevenson

Mayday! Mayday! Anybody here? The emergency signal triggered and my cry for help intensified, but no one could hear it except me. Depleted from the fight, I took my last breath as my insides drowned in disappointment. At the inception of a single thread of discouragement lay a web of bitterness, anger, shame, and offense ready for my entrapment. Imprisoned by my own thoughts, I dared to utter the things that befuddled my mind.

The only place that felt safe to divulge my most intimate thoughts—without judgment—was my journal, so I wrote to release the anguish that shadowed my walk.

Journal Entry #1

I am tired. I am frustrated and I am clueless about what God is doing in my life. The unanswered questions have ushered me into a fragile state of mind and my faith is punctured. My flesh is aroused with feelings of anger and disappointment. Tears are suppressed but on the verge of falling as they await my approval to be released. But I sit here, quietly, motionless, mulling over my emotions trying to control what I will allow myself to feel at this very moment. Don't cry, Dacia! Don't you cry!

My words glared back at me from each page of my misery and I came face to face with a despair that had settled in my soul. It is from these penned thoughts that this book was born … for me, by me, with the intent to save me from me.

The Ugly Truth

True to the nature of the typical man, my husband handled it well; however, I sensed the internal bleeding of a crushed heart as we faced the heartache of another failed attempt. Twenty-eight days had come and gone, again. We sat in complete stillness as the sound of the ticking clock got louder and louder with each breath. It was as if now instead of playing the game of *LIFE*, I was playing a game of *Clue*. I weighed the facts and cross-examined the evidence. The deliberation was not long-lived. The verdict was clear. I was furious with God.

Journal Entry #2

Here You are passing out babies like Santa Claus at Christmas time. And every year I make my list and anticipate unwrapping my precious gift, yet nothing! Have I been naughty? Because my present has yet to appear under the tree and each holiday ends the same … childless. Again, I am forced to enter a new year with the dreams of the last one shattered. The audacity of you to forget me, Your beloved daughter who serves YOU faithfully. What did I do wrong? Do you hear me up there? Matter of fact, are you even real?

The weight of the *wait* was getting heavy and I was on the brink of giving up. Out of offense, God became the Grinch who kept stealing my Christmas. Just like a kid who stopped believing in Santa Clause, I no longer believed that God was a good God.

Yes, I confess. Me, the "super Christian" questioned God's existence. Ensnared by a noose of entitlement, I was ashamed by this newfound discovery that followed my spiritual autopsy, but these were the bleak circumstances that surrounded me at the time. I was defeated with no sign of the light at the end of the tunnel.

As far as I could see, the wheel of life had not spun in my favor and there was no option of clearing the board. No blue or pink pegs can be seen; just my husband and myself circling the board of *life* with a vacant back seat. The wait time was suffocating my hope, which diminished to an all-time low. And like a thirsty baby's empty bottle, I had nothing left!

My willingness to freely express my struggles in my journal became the key to unlocking my own prison. Every page I wrote gave me a little more courage to share my thoughts with others on what felt to be an abysmal situation. I knew there were others silently experiencing the same plight, but to my surprise, the number of people challenged by this issue is staggering. I was far from alone in this thing! So many people, so many different walks of life, and all plagued by this one "dis-ease" that had no discrimination on whom it arrested. INFERTILITY.

Could talking about infertility be a catalyst and remove the weight from my shoulders? Were there any other women forced to digest this unwarranted dose of barrenness and willing to share? Who else questioned the Almighty's existence and found that they too have been accosted by the shame of being an unbelieving believer? An *unbelieving believer*! Does that even exist?

The Naked Truth

At first, I was hesitant about bearing my soul for fear that it would burst the door to judgment wide open. I didn't plan on anyone actually reading my journal entries. It was just my way of expressing myself and venting without inhibitions. I knew some of the entries could come off hypocritical for a Christian. In reading back through them, I cringed at some of the self-righteous things that I had written in the years past. I also do not curse in real life, but boy it felt good to drop a few bombs when penning my anger.

Needless to say, I was living in complete transparency from page to page tapping into every single emotion that surfaced to my flesh. If someone were to pick up my journal to indulge in some late-night reading, I would feel a wee bit embarrassed. Not to mention, several of our family members and friends would have been exposed for their insensitive comments, intrusive questions, ignorant assumptions, and rude insinuations.

However, exposing them would leave me exposed and in my most vulnerable state: bare, butt naked, standing in my own messy truth. Then, everyone would have known my secret. But who cares!

I refuse to shackle myself any longer with the torment of carrying the weight of infertility. My desire is to be free. Free from pain, free from shame, free from judgment, and most of all free from other people's opinions. And, in order to be free, I choose to expose my truth with the certainty that if it is my truth, then it is very well someone else's truth too.

I believe sharing my road to freedom in my waiting season will set some captives free while giving me the absolute pleasure of informing the ignoramus of their ignorance—since clearly, they have no idea that they are offending people with their invasive questions. Just, Nosy!

But we won't fault them for their imbecilic notions—simply pass them this book and point them to the section entitled *Rules of Engagement*. It will enlighten them on how to take better precautions and have a sensitive approach when engaging in casual conversations with people that might be right in the middle of their Waiting Game.

We all have them. What? Seasons of waiting. You might not be able to identify with the despondency of waiting to conceive, but I'm sure you can relate to times when delays felt like denials. Although our waiting seasons may be different, there is one thing I think we can all agree on: the longer we wait in the wings for God to call our number, the tougher it gets to carry the load of frustration. Feeling weighty? Well, let's release the weight together.

Chapter One
The Wait Watcher

First comes love, then comes marriage…

But I was not ready for a baby carriage. After six years of friendship and two years of long-distance courtship, I had the pleasure of marrying my best friend. Albeit ideal for some to jump right into parenthood, I was not ready to trek down that road. A few months before the wedding I began taking birth control pills to ensure we were covered for the honeymoon, which lasted quite a few months as we basked in the introductory stage of our *Happily Ever After*. I had a very vivid vision for my life and what I wanted to accomplish before considering kids, and I was in no rush.

When our three-year-old goddaughter came to visit one summer, "the baby itch" jumped on my husband like the chickenpox! The way he looked at her and the urgency to get home from work to play with her reeked of the "I want one of those" blues. I, on the other hand, must have taken the vaccine because I had not caught the bug. I was just fine being on the *parenthood* waiting list. Don't get me wrong—kids can be adorable, and I loved the idea of having a kid in the home—but I also rejoiced in the fact that we could always return them to their rightful owners. Having little ones of our own was not in the current forecast—at least not for me, not then.

One morning while working in the office, I checked my calendar to glance at projects I had coming up over the next few weeks when I noticed "Anniversary" written and circled in red. Wow! Two years had breezed by and we were now headed into our third year of marriage.

Time was flying like a bat out of hell!

By now, most couples have kicked off into procreation, but it was not a recurring topic in our conversations. I figured we would seriously discuss *children* in years to come. My husband hadn't mentioned it and bet your bottom dollar I hadn't either. It was still "me time."

While reciting the words to a song called "Thy Will Be Done" one morning during my devotion time, I felt this weight of conviction concerning my birth control pills. I can't explain the feeling but there was this unction of the Holy Spirit telling me that I needed to get off my birth control pills immediately.

Wait! What now?

Nah! I'm good!

Not happening! No way!

Theoretically, we should all run in the opposite direction after hearing the side effects that probe the TV screens at the end of every contraceptive commercial. I mean, what's the worst that can happen: blood clots, stroke, heart attack … DEATH?

Usually, I'd take my chances here like everyone else because the hunger for control trumps these harmful side effects any day. Only now, I began to question if "controlling" when I wanted to conceive was my selfish attempt to commandeer the trajectory of my future.

A career in the entertainment industry alludes to the high life, as most see the glitz and glam of working with and for celebrities and assume you've made it—whatever that means—but celebrity adjacency doesn't excuse me from "adulting." I still have bills to pay, just like everyone else.

I was always on the hunt for my next gig. I had achieved some good breaks and was extremely blessed to have gotten as far as I did. In actuality, I hadn't even scratched the surface of my perceived pinnacle.

So, having a baby was an afterthought.

At the end of the day, it's the wife's body and time that is sacrificed at the hand of a growing child. Rarely did I see husbands taking paternity leave after having kids. There never seemed to be a suitable pause—intermission if you will—to allow for the genesis of motherhood to run its course.

Then, there was the added stress of the whole "bounce back" mania to consider. Saran wrapped bellies, waist trimmers, detox teas, and strenuous diets all plaguing our society with an inhumane attempt to get women to drop their baby weight expeditiously—and by any means necessary.

Oh, the pressure!

The more I sat ruminating on what was required of this big step, the more I sparred with this notion of getting off birth control.

Over analytical? Certainly!

Control freak? Absolutely!

As you can see, I surveyed every excuse in the book to maintain my oral contraceptive rituals. With a pouting mouth and tightly crossed arms, I refused to ditch the pills! I was not ready to relinquish that kind of control. I had no intention of letting it go. Nonsense!

Journal Entry #3 (personal conviction)

Nonsense. Who do you think you are, dictating when is the right or wrong time to have children? It's not all about you, dear! There are two people involved in this marriage. Did it ever occur to you that you are being inconsiderate of what your husband wants? The world does not revolve around you. And guess what? Your goals will constantly change. You work in a never-satisfied industry that consistently redefines success based upon the latest trend; therefore, the definition of success will constantly change. You don't get to dictate when's the "right time." That's my job—so get with it!

Was it time? Did I hear God correctly? I questioned my own sanity in this debate with the *Big Man Upstairs*. A fly on the wall would have thought I was losing my mind. Random tears started rolling down my face as I sulked and toiled with this pull in my spirit. Deep down, I knew my husband was ready. He graciously waited for my stamp of approval to start having kids.

That was the thing; I wanted to be in charge of that "start." Getting off birth control would mean I didn't know when that start would actually begin. At any moment I could get pregnant, and I needed to know when, so I could prepare myself—you know—get my head in the game. After all, we are talking about taking on the responsibility of another human being here. My only concern at this time was me, myself, and I. Kids can wait!

No, I'll Wait

I can't lie—I've enjoyed God's favor in my career, doing what I love. With that, came years of sacrifice and persistent pursuit. I wasn't fond of people reminding me of my age or letting me know that "it was time." I began to notice this subtle shame attached to women that chose their career over having children. As if the albatross of the biological clock theory wasn't enough, I also succumbed to a cloud of judgment for choosing to postpone having children.

A family friend told me once, "Girl, go ahead and get you a teaching job or something and give that man some babies." I looked at her as if she had crap on her face. Obviously, she was speaking a foreign language because I did not comprehend. Caught off guard by the comment, the only response I could offer was a curt, "Umm … NO! That is not my calling." Joking or not, it didn't feel good to have people dictating when I should have children or belittling me for choosing to remain on the waitlist.

In Gabrielle Union's interview with *Redbook*[1], she sounded off on the discrimination against working women trying to conceive later in life.

"There's a certain amount of shame that is placed on women who have perhaps chosen a career over starting a family younger. The penance for being a career woman is barrenness. You feel like you're wearing a scarlet letter."

Former supermodel <u>Tyra Banks</u>[2] also spoke about the nostalgia of her younger years on her talk show and what waiting for the "right time" to conceive meant to her. Tears welled up in her eyes when she admitted her anguish:

"For a long time, it was so funny. I was twenty-three years old. I used to tell myself 'in three years I'm going to have kids.' Then, I turned twenty-four, 'in three years I'm going to have kids.' And every single year I just kept saying that. Then after a while, it's like, now I want to, and it's not so easy."

It was evident that she was about to lose it trying to verbalize her pain on live television. The realization of it being *too late is* all too familiar and has sparked conversation as well as controversy, as everyday women determine their route to conception. Tyra Banks was speaking fundamental truth and her experience resonates with those of us in a certain age demographic who desire to have kids in the near future.

I took notice of her grief when she confessed that not having kids was the one thing she regretted in life. Eighteen years had come and gone since she first conceptualized having kids. At the time of this interview, Tyra Banks was forty-one and still childless. Ultimately, she had a child the following year via a surrogate, but this hardly ever negates her subjection to the "it's too late" anxiety. I will never forget her interview because I was immensely moved by her transparency.

As career women, once we decide we are comfortable, stable, secure, and ready to have kids, we don't anticipate trouble conceiving. A family with children was one of my heart's desires along with my husband's. Tyra made me think of the possibility of regrets I might have in fifteen years. I didn't want to wake up one day and realize that we have yet to have kids because I was too busy trying to *be successful*.

I Can't Wait

The conviction that I received in my prayer time resurfaced after watching Tyra Bank's interview. I needed a second opinion to ensure this wasn't a case of insanity. I phoned my friend, Morgan.

Also, freelancing in film and television, I thought she was the perfect person to bounce this sentiment off of. Her sapience surpassed most at our age, so I couldn't wait to hear her interpretation of the madness. She'd been married about a year longer than me, and her husband had also been hinting that he was ready to have children.

I brought her up to speed on Tyra Bank's interview, the epiphany I received about relinquishing control, and my reluctance to follow the instructions that I perceived the Lord had spoken to me. I hurried through, being anxious about her response; although, careful not to miss a bit of detail.

"Hello?" I said, concluding the story with anticipation of her consultation on the matter. The other end of the line began with a pause, followed by a loud breath and I thought to myself, "Ahh, man! This is about to be deep! Lay it on me girl."

"Hmmm!" Morgan moaned.

"What?" I said.

"Lord, Lord, Lord!" she exclaimed.

These vocalized pauses were stressing me out.

"Girl, this word was for me," she finally expressed.

SKERRRRGHHH! My mind screeched like a car hitting the breaks for an unexpected stop. She delicately continued, leery of her word choice.

"This is for me too," she said. "A few days ago, I was convicted of my selfishness concerning my career. This is a revelatory word and I receive what the Lord has confirmed through this encounter that you have experienced."

Well, that wasn't the answer I was looking for; nevertheless, I could tell by her solemnity that she had taken this to heart. She proposed that we continue to pray and ask God for guidance in trusting His plan. We agreed that it was time to have a dialogue with our respective partners, be attentive to their desires, release any personal agendas, and allow God to be God.

We ended our call on a high. Free from burdens with a sense of adventure and an optimistic view of the life ahead of us. I basked in the possibilities and gloated in what I knew would be the joys of motherhood. There was no need to worry about the woes of a "pregnant pause." We can do both—work and have children. This was more than doable.

Giving up our control meant hopping out of the driver's seat and relying on the Creator of Heaven and Earth to lead us down the path He desired for us. That day, we made a pact on the phone that we would surrender to the will of God, embracing this journey to freedom and conception by ridding ourselves of all birth control methods and trusting God's timing.

Two months later, she was pregnant.

Two years later, I was still not pregnant.

Journal Entry #4

... Speechless

"I wanted to write down

Exactly what I felt

But somehow the paper stayed empty

And I could not have described it any better"

-Unknown

Now Wait A Second

"Next month it's going to happen."

"Next year it's all you."

Every month Morgan encouraged me; simultaneously, I wanted to scream, "Shut up already! How many more 'next months' or 'next years' do you have in you? Put a sock in it!"

I knew she was trying her best to be a good friend but after a while, it got painfully awkward. Her heart was in the right place, analogous to mechanical attempts to make me feel better. Instead, these chimes of goodwill made me feel worse, as if she felt sorry for me. I was nobody's charity case. Eventually, as the years continued to pass, it got to the point where we just didn't talk about it. I wanted her to keep her encouraging words to herself, to believe for me in silence because I could not fathom to hear it. God had allowed all of my friends to conceive while I just sat in the queue and watched. I was convinced He had it out for me.

Journal Entry #5

Now wait one second. This $#@% (bleep) just got real. Not one, not two, but three of my closest friends are ALL pregnant. Back to back like dominoes. One month apart from each other. What kind of serendipitous $#@% (bleep) is this? Where's Ashton Kutcher? Bring him out, right now, because I know I am being Punk'd. Did they make a pinky promise behind my back to get pregnant at the same time? No, of course not! That's impossible because they all live in different states and have no relationship with each other outside of me referencing them in conversation. So, what's really going on? This just seems cruel, God. I've been doing everything I know to do: praying, reading, decreeing, declaring, and believing! I guess You are just not answering my calls. Be fruitful and MULTIPLY! That's what Your Word says, right? Evidently, this only applies to certain saints.

Five years into marriage, three years off of birth control and NOTHING. I was starting to think something was wrong with me.

Journal Entry #6

WTF! Still waiting.

Chapter Two
The Waiting Period

My Mind Playing Tricks on Me.

-Geto Boys

Google became my best friend, so I knew what signs to look for; nausea, fatigue, pimples, sore nipples, and bloating. The problem was, some of the signs indicated were a carbon copy to the arrival of *Aunt Flo* lurking around the corner. It made the TWW (two-week wait–the time between ovulation and menstrual cycle) excruciating. My mind played tricks on me every waiting period.

My eagerness to conceive created pseudo symptoms of pregnancy that always resulted in a BFN (big fat negative) and a slipping grip on hope. Misery impregnated my body with every negative test but like clockwork, optimism hurled back in at the kickoff of the next ovulation period. "This could be the month!" was my ongoing pep talk to myself at the end of every cycle.

TWW

I was nearing the close of another TWW (two-week waiting) period and coincidentally my annual exam was scheduled that week. I thought to myself, "How perfect would it be to get a

BFP (big fat positive) while I was at the doctor's office?" Upon her entrance, I unbosomed my woes of conception in hopes of some guidance, on the contrary, I was met with an apathetic nod.

I laid on the table for my breast exam and noticed an unusual amount of soreness and enhanced sensation to the touch. The deeper she probed the more uncomfortable it felt. I didn't recall my breasts ever being that sore. My optimism aroused; I leaned in and coerced a confirmation by commenting that my nipples were awfully sore. She continued with the exam and replied, "Ah okay, you know you are probably…" My eyes lit up in anticipation of some good news-- "about to start your period," she concluded.

What? Every part of me wanted to kick her in the shin and run for giving me that dramatic interlude. According to her, my nipples wouldn't be sore that early if I were pregnant. It was only a sign of PMS (premenstrual syndrome). I rolled my eyes, irked by her deadpan disposition and that cliff-hanging pause.

How would she know anyway, if the signs of PMS and pregnancy are borderline identical? I took into account that she was a doctor and would know; but, then again, doctors get it wrong sometimes. She could have at least offered a kind "it's possible," or "fingers crossed hun"—something a little more promising.

If there was any place I thought safe to unmask my anguish, it was here; but her bland bedside manners made me regret that

I bared my soul to her. She was uninterested and unbothered by my misfortunes. Business as usual for her. Needless to say, I got rid of that gynecologist and was on the prowl for a new doctor.

TTC

Dr. Stone! She was a random pick after searching through our in-network doctors. The complaints of a long wait time took her online ratings down regardless of her remarkable reviews as a doctor, so I decided that she would be the next candidate for my annual exam the following year.

The energy in Dr. Stone's office was warm and welcoming and came with words of affirmation at every turn. It was evident that she believed in setting an atmosphere of *faith*. I was sold!

On my first visit, Dr. Stone was called away because a patient was in labor, so I understood what the wait time fuss on the review board was all about. I came prepared with a book since I was given a heads up on the delays. When she walked in—thirty minutes late—I was greeted by this petite 4'9" diva with shoulder-length hair, a sassy twist, and a fast talk that would send any slow listener into a frenzy. I liked her. I often asked her to repeat herself, but she was pretty thorough making sure that I understood everything she was saying.

She asked the usual twenty-one questions in order to get to know her new patient, and I felt comfortable enough with her to mention my concerns about TTC (trying to conceive). Unlike the previous doc, she was warm and receptive—determined to get to the bottom of this extensive delay of conception. Since it had been a few years with no birth control, she insisted they run tests immediately. One might assume this was an appointment with a fertility specialist but this was an annual exam with a doctor who immediately recognized my distress. First up, blood work.

This wasn't your normal blood draw. Three of those sizable cylinders had to be filled. The nurse pressed my vein with her fingers, draining me of what seemed like all the blood in my left arm before patching me up and sending me off. The results came in rather quickly, and I was back at the office for a follow-up. "Your levels look good, Mrs. Lewis," she said, "now lie back, and let's do an ultrasound to see if there is something internally going on."

This was the first time I had experienced an ultrasound machine. She warned me in advance that the gel was a bit chilly, so I readied myself for the unexpected. In spite of the flinch I offered when the transducer touched my belly, I was amazed by the technology and imagined the day when a child could be seen on the monitor.

Dr. Stone investigated my insides and was able to rule out any pesky fibroids that could be causing some issues with conception. Every good report from her heaved a sigh of relief as the list of possible problems dwindled down. She gave me a wipe to clean myself up and threw her gloves in the hazardous bin. Without looking up from the sink where she washed her hands, Dr. Stone effortlessly asked, "Have you ever had an STI (sexually transmitted infection)?"

"Have I ever had an STI," I repeated—as if I didn't hear her.

She sounded like Charlie Brown's teacher as she explained why she was asking the question. I watched her mouth spewing off in the deep distance as I flashed back to the moment when I got a call.

STI

It was my junior year of college when I went in for a suspicious itch that resembled that of a yeast infection knowing something was off. When it came to my treasures any sign of ailment or questionable symptom was probable cause for me to see the doctor. When the nurse gave me the diagnosis of an STI, understandably I blew a fuse.

The culprit, my boyfriend during that time, not only heard shouts from the top of my lungs with screams of hurt and disappointment but also sensed the abomination of putting my life in jeopardy. I needed someone to blame for this catastrophe but I conceded that ultimately it was my fault for being careless. All he could do was apologize. He knew I hadn't had sex with anyone else and he was exposed for being a liar, cheater and the good for nothing dog that I accused him of. To sum it up, yes, I kindly told him where he could shove the apology, and undoubtedly deleted all traces of him.

He and that STI became a part of my abyss memory bank that I voluntarily zapped with the *Men In Black* neuralyzer, expunging all unwanted memories that could potentially resurface in my head. I didn't want anything reminding me of the incredibly poor decisions I made in my younger years. Regrettably, it looked like my past was trying to haunt my future.

"Yes, ma'am I have had an STI. A very looooooooonnggg time ago," I said, trying to make the best of what felt like the most embarrassing conversation.

Nonchalantly, she continued with her next prognosis as if I said nothing new under the sun. The shame lifted when I noticed the lack of stupefaction in her demeanor. Although an uncomfortable scenario for me to admit, my confession moved her none, which put me at ease.

Sexually Transmitted Infections, unfortunately, are common amongst the population. *The World Health Organization*[3] reports that more than one million STIs are acquired every day.

ONE MILLION!

I believe we all have regrets and a skeleton or two in our closet that we would love to erase from memory and that one is mine. I know some of you may be shocked admittedly, I don't mind the transparency. It's therapeutic and liberating and reminds me of how merciful God is. I was saved by grace and an antibiotic pill that instantly cured it; for that, I am eternally grateful. So, if you didn't make the mistake of assuming you were in a monogamous relationship with a low-down dirty dog, then consider yourself lucky. For me, the lesson learned from an unfortunate situation didn't need to be reminded: the Importance of Safe Sex. Better yet, abstinence.

HSG

"I would like to schedule you for an HSG (hysterosalpingogram) test," Dr. Stone continued.

The *Very Well Family*[4] explains an HSG test as a procedure that involves placing an iodine-based dye through the cervix in order to take x-rays. These x-rays evaluate the shape of the uterus and determine if there is a blockage in the fallopian tubes that would hinder the successful travel of a fertilized egg. Dr. Stone explained that some STIs can cause scar tissue within the reproductive tract, hence the reason for her recommendation that I complete the test.

I reminisced again at my indiscretions. The thought that this idiot from my yesteryear could have compromised my ability to have children sent waves of rage through my veins. Dr. Stone, detecting my concern, reassured me that everything would be fine and that the HSG procedure is one of three exploratory procedures recommended for every couple facing challenges with fertility.

The radiology department was in the same building as Dr. Stone's office. The vivid memory of walking into the procedure room and seeing four nurses was nerve-racking. Why so many? Your guess is as good as mine. In spite of the feeling of intimidation, they were all very kind. One even attempted in her smooth tone to talk me through the procedure, "This may be a bit uncomfortable," which to me meant "this is going to be painful." Euphorically, I remember how it was hard to settle my nerves amid the frigid temperature in the room.

My mind raced as I sat on the exam table. There was part of me that wanted my husband to tag along, yet he didn't offer to take off from work to accompany me to this appointment. Perhaps, he didn't fully grasp the scope of what was going on or he figured I was being overzealous about my health, but it was more than that. The test would determine if my aforementioned recklessness prevented us from having children.

It didn't matter at this point because I was feet-up on the exam table. I slid my foot in the stirrups and attempted to relax my nerves when suddenly, I was startled by a yell towards the glass window behind me.

"She's ready for you doc!" It was one of the nurses cueing the doctor to join the posse.

A tall man with a head full of grays emerged from the connecting room greeting his counterparts with jokes. He had the nurses in an uproar. I assume this was his way of creating a friendly environment and easing the minds of his patients. He was funny so it worked.

After a thorough explanation of what he was about to do, one of the nurses grabbed me and said, "Hold my hand if you need to."

I felt the pressure from the dye fill my uterus creating an intense cramp in my lower abdomen. By far, the most painful bloat I had encountered. I turned my head towards the nurse who had my hand, shut my eyes, scrunched my nose, and let out a moan. As the pressure intensified so did my grip on the nurse's hand. I bet she wished she hadn't offered it because I squeezed the heck out of that joker.

"You're okay. You're okay. We are almost done. Check out the screen!" she said.

The doctor turned the monitor towards me, so I could see the action. I watched the fluid riding through my fallopian tubes like a roaring river. The investigation process was super cool. For a moment, I was able to take my mind off the uneasiness of the cannula in my stomach and revel in the awe of technology.

"You are all clear," the doctor said. "You see that! No blockage Mrs. Lewis. The fluid is flowing just fine."

"YESSSS!!!" I screamed, "Praise the Lord!"

The grim, however, paramount experience was over! When I released the nurse's hand, she gave me a big hug and complimented my patient etiquette. I wanted to hop off of that table and *Moonwalk* my behind right out that door. I was overcome with joy. The doctor and nurses joined in the celebration as the burden of "what ifs" was lifted off of my shoulders.

They insisted that this was the perfect time to go home and get BDing *(baby dancing—a reference to having sexual intercourse during peak fertile windows)*. Evidently, the chances of women getting pregnant significantly increase the following two months after an HSG procedure because the pipes are clean and clear from the dye pushing through the tubes. The nurses bragged as they showed me their *Wall of Fame* with all the baby photos of women who conceived right after their HSG test. How encouraging!

I received a clean bill of health and my reproductive organs were intact, so when I got home, I told my husband the good news and insisted we take advantage of the next two months of BDing on account of my reproductive organs being intact.

And that we did!

WTH

The two-month window came and went. Still nothing. And it seemed like everywhere I looked I was reminded of our glitch.

Journal Entry # 7

I logged on to Facebook this morning and saw a post of a friend announcing her pregnancy. Her post said, "Thank You God for choosing us." What The Hell? Well, I guess that means You didn't choose us. And why is that? Why haven't You chosen us? How do You decide who is worthy and who is not? Is there a lottery pick or random draw? What is Your method to this madness?

There seemed to be no method, just the luck of the draw.

Chapter Three
i'mPatiently Waiting

I'mma need y'all to quit askin' when

Me and my wife gon' have some kids

Right now we just practicin'.

-Andy Mineo

O ur trek to conception—that once brought feelings of excitement—was plunging into hopelessness and I was beginning to self-destruct. It was a slow death, stimulated by the never-ending inquiries and prying questions on our delayed procreation. No matter where we went, family gatherings, friend functions, birthday parties, weddings, baby showers; we could not escape the question, "What is the holdup?"

Chrissy Teigan tackled this topic in an interview one day.

"Why do people ask that question? It is such a personal question and I didn't realize it until I was on the receiving side. But, one day you are going to ask the wrong person when they are having a child and they will pop off on you."

She was right. If you happened to catch me on the wrong day you could expect the uncanny truth of how rude I thought it was for you to ask me when I was having children. And there was no exception for family members especially if I only interacted with them on national holidays.

i'mPolite

It was Resurrection weekend (Easter) and I always looked forward to heading back home for the crawfish boil my husband's family hosts every year. Both of his parent's sides of the family were in town and the crawfish tables were full of people snapping tails. I was eating my crawfish in peace—minding my own business—when out of the blue, my husband's elder cousin decided to put me on blast:

"Say, cousin!" *(I assume he didn't remember or know how to pronounce my name.)* "When y'all gon' have some babies?"

"Are you going to pay for these kids?" I spouted with an impolite tone.

The tail slurping stalled. I felt eyes on me speculating whether I was serious or if the sarcasm was in full effect.

I was dead serious and about-faced right back to the indulgence of my crawfish tail. I said what I said and there was nothing more to say. I was tired of tiptoeing around the subject and I'm sure this cousin learned that day not to ask anyone else that question.

(This doesn't even begin to scratch the surface of the questions I have been asked over the years that made me cringe. Stay tuned because I'll share more of these episodes in the Rules of Engagement.)

I concealed the pain of the mounting years of delays and camouflaged the annoyances of the invasive questions (such as these), and naturally, the load was getting heavier. I was bound to reach my breaking point. I guess today was that day.

I heard a few chuckles after my snappy comeback but my mother-in-law stood silently to my right not missing a beat on her mudbugs. I'm almost certain she was oblivious to our struggle but might have been tipped off after seeing their relative strike a nerve.

My husband's best friend's wife was standing to my left.

She mumbled under her breath, "Girl, I hate when people ask me that question. We are trying to conceive too, so I feel you."

Yup. She was in the secret sorority. Finally, someone who understood my aggravation.

The pressures of these cultural expectations back people into a corner of shame, anxiety, inadequacy, and a slew of other emotional upsets. The weight of it all accompanied by the intrusiveness was becoming a sore spot for me. Questions like this only echo the embarrassment and highlight the shame of the delay. No one is more aware of how long a journey is taking more than the person actually experiencing the prolonged wait.

That being said, seven months had passed since my HSG testing and we were still babyless. Dr. Stone was convinced it was time to move in a different direction.

i'mPerfect

"Mrs. Lewis, since there are no signs of fertility issues with you, I believe that we will need to start the diagnostic procedure for your husband," she said. In an effort to find the culprit that was interfering with conception she prescribed a referral to a specialist for my husband to receive a sperm analysis. "Give this to your husband so that we can start phase two of this process."

"Ok cool," I thought. "This shouldn't be a problem, right?" I was WRONG!

"Nah, Imma chill. I'm not going to the doctor for that. I am a perfectly healthy young man with a moderately good diet and a very active workout regimen," he pontificated. "There is no way I am shooting blanks."

I could smell the arrogance protruding from the certainty in his tone and it irked the hell out of me. I could not understand his logic about refusing to get a semen analysis. And to be quite honest, I deemed it selfish.

Journal Entry #8

Well, that didn't go as planned. I would have come in here and prayed beforehand had I known he was going to be a puffed up butthead. Let me borrow a pin so I can pop his ego real quick. Must I remind him: I'm perfectly fine. It's his turn to get checked … Duh!

What was the big deal? The least he could do was mention it to his general practitioner but no, not a word. To him the idea was stupid, but he conceded and took the referral to shut me up. The paper hibernated on his desk until it collected dust. Every time I glanced at it in passing, resentment grazed my nose. My frustrations mounted and the suppression of my feelings affected my attitude. I needed answers to keep from imploding.

"Why haven't you mentioned to your doctor that it's been years and we have yet to conceive?" I blurted out one evening while dining at one of our favorite spots. "Please help me understand because I am starting to feel a certain type of way about your negligence."

My irresolute husband didn't know what to say.

After a brief moment of silence, he admitted that he was scared. There was a hidden fear in taking the test and he *feared* he could be the problem, that some physical ailment was hindering his swimmers.

At last, a moment of clarity that temporarily soothed my

psyche—although difficult to hear—it was a start. I appreciated his transparency. Incompetence is not a comfortable pill to swallow and from what I understand especially for a man. My nurturing instincts kicked in and consequently encouraged him that we were in this together. I didn't want to put demands on him, so I tried my best to be sensitive to his feelings. Subsequently, I decided I would wait until he felt comfortable with proceeding with his exploratory tests.

i'mPassive

Dr. Stone warned me that this was a delicate situation that had the potential to get messy if the blame game began and she was right! My patience wore thin as the months rolled by. There were times when *Aunt Flo* came, and climatically, a little piece of me wanted to condemn him for his reluctance to get checked out. I didn't want him to resent me for pressuring him, but resentment was inevitable on one end or the other. I could feel the animosity creeping in like a thief in the night.

Journal Entry #9

Last night was rough. Hubby went to bed before me but I had the hardest time falling asleep. I laid in bed seeing another birthday in the horizons and all of a sudden, a wealth of emotions came over me. I started contemplating all of the years we'd been waiting to conceive. This thought of—What if our grandmothers don't get to see our children grow up, due to our infertility—and it broke me. I began to weep uncontrollably, devastated at the possibility of this never happening for us. I tried to disguise my sobbing but by this time it was too late.

My husband, startled by my whimpering, asked if I was okay. I didn't feel like unpacking my baggage, nor did I want to be consoled.

"I'm good," I lied and rolled over.

My true thought was, "LEAVE ME ALONE!" Shortly after rejecting his offer for me to vent, I heard a roaring snore of sweet "zizz" that infuriated me. Here he was soundly counting sheep while I grieved at the possibility of our future. I grew more and more agitated as I felt my empathy was being taken for granted. And in the meantime, he allowed another year to lapse without alluding to any type of plan. Here I believed I was being considerate of his feelings by refusing to pressure him into getting tested and in return, he snoozed this topic for a later date that never arrived. When I reflected on his initial haughtiness on the matter, it aggravated me.

Basically, I was antsy about waiting another year. Can you blame me? My biological clock was ticking and *thirty-five* was coming at me like a freight train!

Out of the blue one evening my husband came home from

work and said, "I am going to the doctor."

"Umm. Ok."

"I've decided to get a sperm analysis," he continued as if he had just come up with this brilliant idea. Yet, my impassivity grew louder.

"What changed your mind?" I murmured.

"Time. I just needed time to reflect and hear from God."

According to him, he was now ready to face the fear of the unknown.

"Ok, cool." My tone was sober because so much time had passed and his enthusiastic declaration to get tested was now met with a callous inflection. All I could think was, "Dang, I wish you had encountered this epiphany half a decade ago." But there we were. Better late than never.

Chapter Four
The Waiting Room

When the train goes through a tunnel and the world gets dark, do you jump out? Of course not. You sit still and trust the engineer to get you through.

-Corrie ten Boom

I probed my husband the entire ride to his appointment. "What are you thinking?" "How are you feeling?" "Are you all right?" The anguish in his "I'm fine" response led me to believe that there was panic, a fear that he didn't want to express. Then again, maybe that was my anticipation projecting feelings on him.

We walked into the huge glass doors and were greeted by an elevator attendant.

"How may I help you?" he said, cutting off his conversation with the security guard.

"Doctor Bloom's office," my husband stated.

"The Reproductive Clinic is on the fifth floor," the attendant replied, directing us to the elevators.

I didn't need him to announce it to the masses. Seriously, did he have to be so boisterous? He might as well have hollered,

"Got trouble having a kid? This way!"

Thanks for your discretion, sir. NOT!

My sweaty armpits are always an indicator that my nerves had kicked into high gear. I felt the water dripping down my side. The oversized automatic doors to the Reproductive Clinic swung open and all eyes glanced towards us. The loudness of the doors alarmed the room of incoming traffic, jolting me into what felt like the catwalk of infertility.

What appeared to be an ecstatic welcome from the receptionist during sign in, some would call polite customer service, conversely, I assessed it as a pitiable effort to empathize with patients. I knew my over-critical synopsis was nothing short of embarrassment seeping through my well-assembled facade of confidence.

The waiting area was nowhere near empty. One would think there would be some comfort in knowing you weren't the only one going through this, but there was no solace in this visit. The entire room looked to be on edge. During the wait, I proceeded to size up everyone, wondering what ailment inflicted each patient. I diagnosed every patron as if I was the expert, and created a story in my head from a mere glance at their demeanor, respectively.

One man, looking to be in his early thirties, sat upright in his chair twirling his wedding band as he stared at the tufted carpet. He squirmed in his seat just enough to adjust his posture but never lifted his gaze from the floor. He was nervous, which made me nervous. I brushed it off as the uniform anxiety of sitting in the waiting area of a reproductive clinic. Not knowing what was on the other side of the waiting room door is sure to have anyone shook. It plagued me too, but I found contentment in convincing myself that we were only there for a routine check-up.

As we foresaw, it was a pretty standard appointment. My husband's doctor ran some tests, drew blood, and we were out. Effortless. Our next step was the WAIT.

The Diagnosis

I had the luxury of celebrating my birthday in Pescara, Italy, and while at dinner with my husband I mentioned quite a bit of time had passed with no word about his results. We surmised that no news was *good news*. I guess telepathic waves traveled back to the states because while traveling from Pescara to Rome, the following day, our festivities were pulverized by a call from Dr. Bloom. I was anxious to hear what was being relayed to my husband on the other end of the phone as I witnessed his countenance change.

He ended the phone call and relayed the message.

"The results showed my sperm motility and the count was significantly low," he said, "and Dr. Bloom is recommending I come in for further testing."

Whoa! I wasn't expecting that. What was I expecting? I guess, ideally, I would have liked to hear that his tests were great and we were just being summoned to play a round of the *waiting game* with God. I was blown away at this news, be that as it may, I secured a poker face to avoid adding to the disgruntled atmosphere. Whether 100% accurate or not, my husband's worst nightmare came true.

Our bus ride to the Eternal City that was previously full of chuckles and grins flipped into a quiet voyage of cogitation as the open fields of Italy offered no comfort. It was apparent that our sprint to conception was turning into a marathon.

Journal Entry #10

I'm not going to lie, when we got the news from his doctor, I was like—I'm free! It isn't me! Under no circumstances am I gloating at the misfortune that was dealt to my husband but I felt some consolation. At the same time, I feel horrible for my husband. I believe women are more equipped for emotional battles like these. I can handle the secret cries, and temper tantrums on the floor asking God why. But after each failed attempt I strap my gloves back on, and hop in the ring, ready for the next bout. It's what I've been doing for the past few years anyway. I've been drowning in disappointment, so I can handle his too. I would much rather my womanhood be in query than for him to feel incompetent, carrying the burden of this hardship.

The Prognosis

Our trip home from Italy was greeted with a follow-up visit to Dr. Bloom for my husband's second sperm analysis. We hoped to get a more positive report on the new results but the numbers proved true. For lack of better words, my husband was indeed "shooting blanks." Some unknown entity was inhibiting the performance of his sperm thus lowering our chances of achieving pregnancy.

Dr. Bloom concluded that my husband was suffering from varicoceles, which are swollen varicose veins in the scrotum area. These enlarged veins can cause low sperm production, decrease sperm motility, and increase sperm deformation. Simply put, they damage or kill sperm.

Dr. Bloom suggested that outpatient surgery was presumably the best option for my husband. However, there was not a definitive answer regarding the sole impediment, and no guarantee that surgery would boost his count or increase our chances of conception. The other two options were assisted techniques. One method is Intrauterine Insemination (IUI), which entails placing the sperm in the uterus. The second is In Vitro Fertilization (IVF), which involves placing the sperm in the egg and then transferring the embryo to the uterus. All are viable options used to facilitate and expedite fertilization.

They all sounded dreadful at first mention and after hearing the costs of the procedures, the frightening look on my face prompted Dr. Bloom to present a fourth option.

"Or you could proceed with meticulously timed intercourse, nutritional supplements, and OPKs (ovulation prediction kits) and we can reconvene in a few months," he stated.

Following the heartbreaking prognosis, my husband didn't speak about the next steps, so I tread lightly on the subject. I knew this was a blow to his ego, so I refrained from badgering him to decide what to do for fear of trampling whatever confidence he had left. Ultimately, my thought was to let him lead on this one.

We resorted to holding off on any aggressive methods and kept pursuing the natural route. He was adamant to walk it out, believing God for supernatural healing and childbirth until he felt the Lord reveal something different. I just went along for the ride. We quoted scriptures, prayed prayers of faith, and declared words of affirmation over our situation. Vacations were planned with execution in mind, scheduled intercourse dates were set, and OPKs were stocked. We were on a mission and paired our prayer life with intentional action, but in spite of our efforts, we were met with challenges that eventually unraveled my faith.

Still Waiting

Aunt Flo had left the building, so I knew ovulation was approaching. Once again optimistic about another stab at getting our BFP, I ran to the store to grab an OPK since we ran out. I scanned the aisle for other products that might enhance our chances and saw a box that read as follows: fertility-friendly lubricant, a high-quality lubricant that mimics cervical fluids to support the sperm journey.

"Hmm, something to help the swimmers swim," I thought, "interesting."

I grabbed my phone in search of approval ratings. The reviews looked good, so with that in mind I was pumped to try a water-based substance that would help make a smooth ride while increasing our fertility chances. I dropped it into my cart and continued browsing the shelves until the eagerness of a teenage girl skipping down the aisle captured my attention. More intriguing was who followed behind her, a budding male with a grin from ear to ear. I smiled at what looked like puppy love. Notably, the realization of purpose succumbed me, "Why are they on this aisle? Oh lord! The lovebirds are grabbing condoms. Don't do it!"

Nevertheless, I chuckled at my mental attempt to save these young bucks from my past mistakes, I reached for an OPK only to be thwarted by the girl's grab for a pregnancy test below it. My eyes got big.

"No way!" I shouted inside. She couldn't have been older than twenty. Annoyed by her *luck* I gave a posed smile that immediately dropped as I passed them and rushed to check out.

"Really God," I snarled under my breath.

Dismissing my fleeting moment of envy, I scurried home to take the ovulation test which yielded a happy face. It was time. I continued researching my new product. This lubricant was highly rated not just for the success of conception but for enjoyment, and who doesn't want to make their BD more enjoyable.

The hubby and I only managed to hit our scheduled date once this week, so we had to nail it that day. No exceptions.

I called my husband to get his estimated time of arrival from work as the sun was nearly set for the evening.

"Hey, are you on the way home?"

"No, I'm still here," he replied. We have a few problems that we are trying to solve, but they should be fixed soon."

"Okay, see you soon."

I decided to watch a few of my recorded shows to pass the time while simultaneously doing more extensive research on my new helpmate for the night—the lubricant. Startled by a Star

Wars commercial, I jumped up. Evidently, I fell asleep, phone-in-hand. I looked at it and said, "10:30? WHAT!" Below the time there was a text that said "still here" that came in at 10 p.m. The anger began to rise up in my bones.

Not again! Livid at the text I just read, I told Alexa to dial hubby. Attempting not to let my grievance seep through the phone, I momentarily altered my demeanor,

"Hey, you okay?" I said.

"Hey babe, yeah we are still trying to fix a machine. I am going to be here for a while, don't wait up!"

My husband works on all kinds of machines for a living. I am certain they have a mind of their own. It was as if those frantic machines would intentionally throw a wrench into our plans. Every time ovulation week arrived, they would fail, causing my husband to work sixteen-hour days.

"Okay, I'll put the food up," I responded graciously as to not add to his stressful day.

"DON'T WAIT UP!" I thought after I ended the call.

"What do you mean don't wait up? It takes two to Tango."

"UGHHH!" I screamed, storming down the stairs.

I walked into our room and slumped into bed. I recalled the girl in the store with her boyfriend purchasing a pregnancy test and cried myself to sleep. It all seemed so *unfair.*

The creak of the bedroom door prompted me to wake up and look at the clock. It was 1 a. m. when I was greeted by my husband. Though dissatisfied with his tardiness, I pushed aside my disdain and reasoned that we could still make good use of this fragile window of time.

While he showered, I quietly rushed into another bathroom to insert a small amount of lubricant, keeping in mind that the users say too much makes for a sloppy environment. Quickly returning to bed, I awaited his arrival to join me for some cuddle time. Thankful that he made it home safely, I laid my head on his chest and rested there for a minute. When I leaned in for a kiss to initiate the task at hand, I was greeted with a raucous snore.

Are you kidding me?

My knee-jerk reaction was to shake him silly until he pulled it together. I abruptly recognized my insensitive efforts and said good night as I rolled over to the other side of the bed. Mission aborted. There goes another one. Another missed opportunity—better luck next time.

Chapter Five
The Waiting Game

Losing heart is the most dangerous thing. You can put any obstacle in front of me and I will jump over it. But when you lose heart, you lose everything.

-Meryl Streep

Unfortunately, the next time, often became the *next time*, and missed opportunities became the norm. Days turned into months, and months into years and everyone in our inner circle had conceived at least once, thus isolating us as the unrevealed barren couple. When asked when we were having kids, I was able to mask with confidence an abrupt, "in due season," successfully bamboozling the masses into thinking I was completely unbothered by our inability to conceive. Even though I mastered the art of saving face, my insides burned with the pangs of despondency.

I chose to independently carry the weight of the barrenness, leaving no one to combat the thoughts that circulated my mind, not even my husband. But in isolation, I voiced my disgruntlement with God, told Him it was not fair and begged Him to honor my request to conceive. Driven to despair by the echo of my own voice I was convinced that God had a mean streak and deliberately turned a deaf ear toward my prayers. As

His silence grew so did mine and out of that estrangement, a whirlwind of agnosticism was born. Unbelief was slowly creeping in and a waiting-war was waged on a vital tool that was created to sustain me—Hope.

Hope Deferred

We exhausted ourselves trying to hit the bullseye. Even with perfectly timed vacations during the fertile window and a redundancy of BDing, we still came up short. Whether a targeted hit with no success or an epic miss altogether, even a well-thought-out plan to natural conception proved to be difficult on all fronts.

My hope that this would happen for us had now decimated. I tried to muster up the strength to pray for myself, but I had no words, even for God.

Journal Entry #11

What's the use of praying if God doesn't answer? Clearly God is not here for my $#@% (bleep).

But if God did have an answer, was I really open to hearing it? I was stuck in a quagmire of grief, anger, disappointment, and bitterness. The emotional bondage left me feeling deserted by

God. I convinced myself that if we got pregnant, great, but I was no longer "trying" to conceive. Oh, the lies we tell ourselves to shield us from further disappointment.

I was so entangled in discouragement and entitlement that I wasn't able to recognize the signs of a broken heart. Assuming God had dismissed me, I was offended and a sense of abandonment had seeped in. All that I thought I knew about God was now in question.

Journal Entry #12

So, I have a question ... What's the purpose in striving to live a righteous life when it seems like those that serve you faithfully are those that face implausible opposition? I've witnessed faithful servants barely getting by while wicked evil people sit on goldmines. I see captivating men and women believing You for marriage yet they're single and advancing in age with apprehension. And then there's parents killing and abusing their kids while the most incredible couples yearn to have a child of their own. It all seems so backwards. And when I sit here and ponder on what is clearly unfair, it makes it all too easy to question this religious piffle. I'm over it.

Heartsick

My routine prayer life suffered and eventually came to a screeching halt. Before long, I was wandering in a wilderness of hopelessness and flirting with agnosticism. No one knew it except me, although I'm sure my husband saw my shift to skepticism. I would hurl sarcastic remarks on God's existence when my husband broadcasted his faith. Apart from him I had the people fooled and I wore the guise of a believer by attending church regularly, tithing, and even encouraging people experiencing turmoil to trust in God. For some reason, I believed God for everyone's situation but my own; the epitome of an *unbelieving believer*—a walking, talking oxymoron.

During that time, if someone were to ask me if I believed in God, I honestly don't know how I would have responded. "Blasphemy," some might say. No, not at all. I was just at a point in my life where the *weight* of the *wait* became so taxing that I was uncertain about whether God existed. There were so many doubts in my head that it was hard to grasp the truth. I finally understood how people could give up on God as this dubious mindset caused me to retreat from my spiritual walk. In some way, I felt that I was punishing God by choosing not to commune, but in actuality, I was punishing myself.

A War-Torn Soul

The end of a calendar year tends to be everyone's time to reflect and evaluate the previous twelve months of life. For us, it was a reminder of our stroke of bad luck.

My husband sat on the couch staring at a blank TV screen wondering why God would ignore our supplication for kids.

"I never thought it would be us going through this," he said. I detected the frustration in his voice. I could see him gnawing on the pain, the confusion, the unanswered questions, and the "why me."

The tides were turning and it was now an open season on his faith. Seeing him hurt made me want to help. I aimed to encourage my husband as much as I could, but I was spiritually dull—still deliberating God's very existence. With a deep desire to be my husband's savior, I couldn't help him because I was wounded, and I needed to help myself first. I needed to stop the hemorrhaging of my own spirit.

How? The open wounds were far from healed and I didn't know how to make the bleeding stop. I was trapped in a matrix of spiritual uncertainty and ashamed to admit that after a lifetime of Christianity, I was now straddling the fence. A study done by the Barna Group[5] indicated that when self-proclaiming Christians, like myself, were faced with spiritual doubt, they halted their spiritual routines. This poll showed that two-thirds of Christians surveyed stopped praying, reading the Bible, and attending church when their faith was tested.

It proves the scripture true: *Hope deferred makes the heart sick* (Proverbs 13:12); so when Christians feel slighted by God, there can be a tendency to withdraw rather than draw closer to Him. Without the proper foundational structure in place to help you sustain, the unrelenting disappointments can make even the strongest heart sink and fail.

Bishop T.D. Jakes describes it as falling "into the abyss of wanting absolutely nothing because sometimes, it is easier not to want anything than it is to want it and not get it." I can sum it up in one word—Hopelessness. It's when you arrive at the desolate place of no expectation or anticipation of things working in your favor. Unbeknownst to most, this feeling of forlornness is a silent killer—the breeding ground for depression.

Journal Entry #13

I stood in the bathroom this morning staring at myself in the mirror. Motionless, empty of thoughts and full of pain. The longer I looked, the more intense the anger grew inside of me. Suddenly, I felt this dismal aura as the presence of darkness engulfed the room. The enemy assailed my head with thoughts of worthlessness. I questioned my purpose ... my existence ... and perpended if my living was totally in vain.

It's fair to say that my disposition was off for quite some time, and although this may be true, on that day, my husband had an indicator that alerted him to my defeatism. Right when I walked out of the bathroom he said, "We are more than conquerors through Christ Jesus."

I took a lungful breath and exhaled all of the pent-up

emotions. I cried in my husband's arms, expunging the disarray that tormented my soul. These bottled up feelings of uncertainty resulted in a spiritual suicide and something had to give.

God, being the omniscient God that He is, will sometimes send a messenger to provoke your spirit. In this case, after he sent my husband to encourage me, He sent Dr. Tony Evans' sermon to convict me:

"Don't get so caught up in what God hasn't done for you that you forget all that God has done for you."

Yup! Thought-provoking indeed! I bowed my head in both shame and gratitude. Tears streamed down my face as I reminisced on all the times God spared my life. In my heart, I knew God was real based upon the simple fact that I am still breathing. The fact that I'm still breathing also reaffirms that God is good. We all have forgotten God's grace when burdened by an unexplainable season that's layered with severe disappointments. Society has made it easy to forget too because we buy into the law of cause and effect and its implication on our lives. Given that, some things defy that law. God is one; His timing is another.

There is false pretense that doubt is a negative thing but the Editor in Chief of Barna Group[6], Roxanne Stone, explained it as such:

Spiritual doubt has been a reality of the Christian journey since the disciples—and today is no different. Just like first century Christians, their twenty-first-century counterparts question aspects of their theology, doubt the existence of God and mourn his seeming absence during hard times. Doubt remains a flip side on the same coin as faith. For the majority of Christians, this inevitable doubt is a catalyst to spiritual growth. This should lead pastors and spiritual mentors to view seasons of spiritual doubt in their constituents as fertile soil—not as dangerous ground.

Clearly there was a lesson to be learned in my extensive pilgrimage—maybe God wanted to unveil the areas of my life where trust and growth were mandatory. That would require me to stop back-pedaling away from God and, instead, search for His presence in the midst of my affliction.

So, one morning, after a lengthy spiritual sabbatical, I paid God a visit:

Journal Entry #14

Well God, I know it's been a while. I've been struggling with this whole faith thing. I've denounced prophetic words and refused to believe that You are good because of my anger and offense. I ask for forgiveness. I'm not sure how I got into this rut but I know I need help getting out. Give me clarity and revelation on what You are trying to teach me during this waiting season. I'm not sure what is required of me but I'm willing to put forth the effort of building a more intimate relationship with You. Reveal the areas of my heart that need healing and deliver me from the snares of disappointments.

If God wouldn't answer my questions about conception, then I'd settle for a quest to undo the disconnect that left me unable to process His goodness in the midst of this gloom. At least my *War-Torn Soul* would be slightly relieved of its agony.

Chapter Six
Wait For It

He is a wise man who does not grieve for the things which he has not,

but rejoices for those which he has.

-Epictetus, Fragments of Epictetus

On the upside of this expedition lay the closing on our new house. This was our first huge purchase as a couple and I couldn't wait to decorate. There is no doubt about it, shopping makes you happy and I'd go as far as to say it helps keep you sane—just saying.

Once we settled into the new area my husband was on the hunt for a new church home. He loathes traffic and the commute to our previous church had become a bit lengthy and that's before factoring in the big city congestion. I advocated for watching church online because if I was disinclined to attend service, a simple click of the mouse and *poof* it's gone; but my husband wasn't having that. Every Sunday—we go to church (our feelings don't get a vote). He probably thought that dragging me to church every Sunday would inevitably rekindle my fire for the Lord.

My husband's coworker mentioned that her church added a location on our side of town. The following Sunday we ventured out to their new campus and get this: it was only seven minutes away from our house. Of course, the seven-minute commute had my husband at *Hello*.

Prior to the pastor taking the stage, his wife walked up and prefaced the sermon with a prayer for her husband and the word that was to come forth from him. It was like nothing I had ever seen or heard before. Her words blazed the stage with passion. It was electrifying. Give me a sip of whatever she drank that morning because the juice she had was legit. "I want to pray like that for my husband," I thought. The boldness, urgency, and fire jumped off the stage and lit up the room. I just knew, after that prayer, her man was about to tear the roof off the joint.

What captivated me most about her prayer was the continual reference of God as Daddy. "Daddy, You are ... and Daddy we are ... and Daddy have Your way in this place!" It was a peculiar label to me, but the vigor in her confession of faith was so powerful that I was convinced she had God's ear. In my thirty-odd years on earth, I don't think I've ever referred to God as *Daddy*. As she interchanged the words—*God* and *Daddy*—in the same breath, I was hung on the affection that accompanied her cry.

There seemed to be a running theme here because the choir sang "Good Father" during praise and worship. God had my undivided attention as I tried to decode this *Daddy* theme that was provoking my spirit. It wasn't until later in my prayer time that I realized this was the revelation that I had asked for. God was dismantling my perspective on who He was to me. Stay with me now because this was a profound moment that changed the trajectory of my relationship with God and broke mental chains that I didn't even know existed.

What Daddy?

My mom and dad never married, so I did not have the opportunity of growing up with my biological father. When my mom found out she was pregnant with me she opted out of continuing the relationship with my dad. It was the best decision she could have ever made, as I have a half-sister that is two-and-a-half weeks older than me. Do the math and chew on them apples for a moment. Exactly! Papa was a rolling stone. (Moving on!)

This might sound weird to some, but when I was younger I never desired a father-daughter relationship with my dad. There was a missing link there that I never appraised as a necessity in order to live a good life. Part of that is because my mom is a superwoman, so I never felt a parental void of any kind.

Now on the flip side of that coin, I did take issue with trusting people who were infamous for lack of follow-through due to a few episodes with my biological father. I was constantly let down by his immature antics, which resulted in my cutting back on communication with him at a very early age. He was a perpetual liar, in my book. He made false promises that never proved true, so my withdrawal was stemmed by his constant failure to commit to his word. It was my sophomore year of college when I gave up on building any type of functional relationship with my dad.

My first year at school was financially covered thanks to scholarships. Every other semester my mom made it her duty to ensure tuition was paid. I was going to be the first in my immediate family to graduate from college, so it was a "by any means necessary" approach. I ended my freshman year on the Dean's list, not because I was so focused, but because I had to redeem a disastrous first semester—*we'll blame that on acclamation, not procrastination.*

Nevertheless, my mom bought me a new car at the top of my sophomore year, although I am not convinced it was because I made the Dean's list. Between me and you, I think it was because she was tired of taking that seven-hour, round trip drive to my university for every holiday break—or random homesick episode. With a car payment now on my mom's list of bills, you can imagine that funds were tight that year. So, my books were now my responsibility. Those of you familiar with college costs know how expensive books can be; even a used book was a pretty penny. My mom suggested that I reach out to my dad to help cover the expense.

Reluctantly, I obliged and called my dad to ask for

assistance. When he answered the phone, I explained my dilemma and eagerly he said, "No problem, I will put a check in the mail tomorrow."

I thought to myself, "Man, that was way too easy. Could he actually come through this time?" You see, I was skeptical due to his past untruthfulness, but I had hoped that he'd turned over a new leaf—you know, a "come to Jesus moment." Maybe this was it.

A few days rolled by, a week came and went, still no check in my mailbox. This was looking sketchy. I called him to inquire of its status and he guaranteed the check was on the way. After a couple of weeks passed, I dialed his phone number with fuming force, determined to let his lying behind HAVE IT.

Seconds after, he answered the phone, he said, "You still haven't gotten the check? I sent it a while ago."

I waited to hear the rest of his spiel, and what I heard next struck a chord that would replay in my mind for years to come. He blurted out, "Goddammit! That old crackhead must have gone into my mailbox and stole your check! Wait until I see his @$$."

Come on! A crackhead? Lies and deception!

I held the phone, outraged by his bogus rubbish. You mean to tell me a crackhead stole a check with someone else's name on it? Wow, he could have conjured up a better lie than this preposterous fabrication.

I was used to the broken promises but this was one for the books. Literally. Tears welled up and I sat there in utter disbelief.

"Alright, talk to you later!"

Click! I slammed the phone down—*back when you could ACTUALLY slam a phone down*. I was DONE.

Even though I knew this was a bald-faced lie, a part of me wanted to believe the hype so it wouldn't hurt as bad.

The audacity to hoodwink your own daughter!

The influx of previously broken promises catalyzed the dissolution of our relationship, but this was the straw that broke the camel's back. That day he lost all of my respect and what title he did have as my dad. He became nothing but a sperm donor that I called by his first name. Out of pity, I recall checking on him every couple of years. But for the most part, I disengaged from him, severing ties with minimal communication if any.

I found that distance was the best way to protect myself from any further disappointment and broken promises. Sound familiar? Let me expound.

In the Bible, we literally see where God has made thousands of vows. Some vows are His promises to do something, give something, or bring something to pass. There are even vows for what God will not do. These commitments from God can seem like broken promises when they don't manifest within our time frame. In turn, this can result in us feeling like God is a liar. Unfortunately, this mindset is framed from our experiences on earth with the fickleness of mankind.

I came to the realization that I was struggling to see God as a good Father because of the let-downs. The failed pregnancy attempts felt like broken promises, which were contradictory to what I read in God's Word. When the disappointments mounted, I headed into survival mode by forfeiting communication with God to protect myself from the likelihood of any more pain. It wasn't a blatant disrespect toward God; it was an immature reflex that was initiated by my natural experiences with my earthly father.

My dad didn't do what he said so I withdrew. God hadn't done what His word said so I pulled back. It became evident that I had some natural daddy issues that bled over into my spiritual relationship.

With this discovery, God was exposing that—yes—I knew Him as Creator, Miracle Worker, and El Shaddai. I even knew Him as King of Kings and Lord of Lords, among many other names of the great I AM. However, in knowing all of that, I felt no confidence in Him as my Father—the one who loves, protects, and cares for me; the one I could count on for anything. Abba Father, the one who cannot and will not lie because it is not in His nature to do so (Numbers 23:19). This is the essence of God that He wanted me to be acquainted with.

God longs for us to know that He is good even when it doesn't feel good. No matter what circumstances we face, God's character is unchanging; much different than the temperament of human nature.

Journal Entry #15

Daddy,

Forgive me for placing Your character on the same playing field of the faulty character of my earthly father. Forgive me for categorizing Your love for me in the same realm as that of a man. Take away my misconceptions about You. I want to experience Your nature and character. Help me get to know You as Daddy, My Good Father so that I can lay my head on Your chest and experience Your love for me like never before.

I started reading and meditating on the Gospels, to reacquaint myself with God's unfailing love and ultimate sacrifice, His Son! The more I saturated myself in God's word the harder the enemy tried to probe my thoughts. Late nights and early mornings were the enemy's opportune time as the pressures of sadness and desolation hovered my bed insisting that God was being good to everyone except me.

But I pressed in harder, spending a lot of time in prayer in order to build my faith and allow God to heal the broken areas of my heart.

With a growing faith, a fresh revelation, and a willing spirit, I released my complaints and shifted my focus to intentionally sow into the very thing I didn't have—kids!

Great Expectation

Ten, nine, eight, seven, six, five, four, three, two, one, Happy New Year! The ringing sound of the new year came in right smack dab in the middle of our living room floor watching *Dick Clark's New Year's Rockin' Eve*. Together, my husband and I sang and danced to the tunes of the previous year then bowed our heads for a moment of prayer. The refreshing scent of a blossoming new year brought gratitude and a new perspective of the life ahead of us. The next morning, I headed straight to my office, grabbed my journal, and communed with my Father.

Journal Entry #16

Daddy,

You are gracious and kind to me. I thank You for another year on this earth. My desire is to trust You wholeheartedly. You don't owe me anything. Instead of focusing on what I don't have, help me to rejoice at what I do have. I am ready to embark upon this new season of my life. What can I do for You, Lord? Here I am, You can use me.

The past few years were clouded with my selfish ambitions and complaints but thank God I was able to refocus the lens and make every day count toward the end goal of impacting and inspiring others.

Early on in my career as a professional dancer and choreographer, I discovered that my gift is encouraging others to pull out the greatness within and believe God for the impossible. That audacious faith was the spark that ignited the dawn of my career and I had the testimonies to prove it.

A creative freelancing career in itself is a test of faith that requires me to believe for the next job without seeing it in advance. I can only give credit to the *Man Upstairs* who gives me the key ingredients that keep me afloat: prayer, praise, perspective, and perseverance.

I longed for the day to teach my kids the importance of each of these components and tell them all the miraculous stories of how God moved in my life. From the divine favor and supernatural breakthroughs to life lessons that shook me to my core, I was anxious to share them all and possibly help my kids avoid some of the pitfalls and potholes that impeded my journey. But the Lord revealed to me that I didn't need to wait to have my own children. There were plenty of kids who could use that insight.

Later that year I started a mentorship program through my company D.O.P. Entertainment (Different On Purpose). I knew that if I could render to the next generation the significance of an unrelenting faith and an unstoppable mindset, the sky would be the limit for them. The next several months of my life were dedicated to educating, motivating, and inspiring young artists who aspired to thrive in music, television, and film.

My goal was to help each student in the program build a solid foundation and equip them with the tools necessary to attain, by faith, every goal that they set out to accomplish. Through the Holy Spirit, I was able to speak life to their dreams and usher them into their full potential. It became a ministry to me. I wanted to make sure that every artist, performer, and future influencer who crossed my path knew that this road was not going to be easy, but an uphill battle that only the strong in mind, body, and spirit would survive.

Practice What You Preach

So much of my time was spent cultivating and executing the program, that I didn't have time to wallow in the woes that raided my mind. In a sense, my mentees were my newly adopted children and a priority in my life. Their growth and well-being were important to me. My heart was getting a crash course on the selflessness that accompanied motherhood.

I challenged them to walk out of mediocrity and into greatness. This required them to take bold steps of faith, and if I could achieve this level of success doing what I loved, so could they. Therefore, I drowned them with information requiring them to read books and do homework in addition to their routine grade schoolwork. Teaching them and seeing their growth was invigorating. I was optimistic about the possibilities of not only their lives but mine as well.

Isn't it funny that sometimes the advice you give to others is the very advice you need yourself? I know God has a sense of humor, so it doesn't surprise me that I was one of the mentees in my own mentorship program. I was helping others and exposing the severity of my own unbelief in the process. The faith principles that I was teaching my mentees were treasures I had chosen to compartmentalize by only believing God in certain areas of my life: conception not being one of those areas.

What's the saying? "Practice what you preach," right? Hmph!

Lord knows I swear by that phrase. Because I loathe hypocrisy, I had to ingest a dose of the medicine that I had prescribed to my students. I was forced to take a hard look in the mirror, and it reflected back at me revealing that I didn't believe my own hype. I now had to accept that the relentless spirit I was lecturing on was lying dormant in my own life. But this was my call to bulldoze through the disappointments that left me stagnant in my belief for children.

Despite my temporary withdrawal and anger with God, anything was possible; and it was time to start tapping into the same indefatigable faith I was teaching and practice what I was preaching.

Chapter Seven
Wait A Minute!!!

Sometimes the answer to prayer is not that it changes life,

but that it changes you.

-James Dillet Freeman

The ten-month mentoring program was nearing an end. Their final showcase was less than a month out and my head was spinning along with my schedule. I barely noticed that my cycle was a few days late. My nipples were not sore at all and that big pimple that rears its ugly head on the side of my cheek didn't have its normal visitation hours. I paid it no mind, assuming the chaos from planning the showcase caused *Aunt Flo* to delay her arrival to the party; but, two weeks later she was still a *no-show*. By now my nipples were unbearably tender. I vaguely remembered my mom mentioning she knew she was pregnant when she cringed at the discomfort of the water hitting her breast in the shower.

I told my husband that I was two weeks late, so we decided it was time for a pregnancy test. With minimum enthusiasm shown, he went to the store, got two pregnancy tests, put them on my desk in my office, and went back downstairs to finish his *honey-do list*. About an hour later I went to the bathroom, sat on the toilet, peed on the stick, set it on a napkin, put it on the side of the tub, and scampered to my prayer closet to pass the time. I felt confined in the closet, so I paced the floor of my office instead. Anything to avoid sitting in the bathroom during the wait. I was nervous, mostly because I was scared of my hopes plummeting down the drain. However, I braced myself for the results.

I walked in the bathroom, glanced down and saw the word PREGNANT on both tests. A shiver ran up my spine as I stood in absolute disbelief. It was my first BFP, but where was the back-slapping joy I thought I'd feel? Instead, I locked in a trance with chills permeating my body. I cried, but I don't think they were blissful tears, more like tears of terror and lamentation for life as I knew it.

Was I ready for this?

I Knew It!

I grabbed my phone to shoot a video to commemorate the occasion. However, my hair wasn't done, so I thought it might be a good time to throw on a wig—just in case I decided to show someone the video or post it to social media. Narcissistic? Maybe, but don't be judgy now. In this day in age, it is imperative for a girl to have three things accessible at all times: a red lip, some mascara, and a wig. These were essential for a last-minute put together and I wasn't going to savor this moment on video with a disheveled mop on my head.

I ran downstairs to tell my husband, who had completely forgotten that he had purchased the test.

"It's positive!"

"You're lying!" he replied, awestruck.

"Nope. It's positive." I said as I parked myself on the stairs.

We sat there and laughed, I cried, we laughed some more while trying to make sense of what became the biggest surprise of our lives. How it happened was a complete mystery to us—besides the obvious. There were no OPKs, no timed intercourse, no charting, just us enjoying each other. We made a conscious decision not to be consumed by TTC, and somehow, we unintentionally hit the bullseye.

Journal Entry #17

Wait a minute! I wasn't ready, Homie. We took a test last night and honestly God I must say I didn't expect a YES. I'm excited—I think. Way to throw a bombshell. I'm surprised but I'm not surprised because I prayed that You'd blow my mind this season. Of course, a part of me is still in shock and a bit confused. I guess I've gotten so used to NO that it's hard to believe the YES. I don't know if I'm thrilled or having anxiety. Peace be still, Dacia. Lord, help me to embrace this with open arms. I am believing You for a smooth and pain-free (if possible) pregnancy and 100% healthy child. Amen.

Some of you might think I'm a little looney and others will immediately recognize it as the prophetic when I say this, but— I KNEW IT! I had this knowing in my gut, this supernatural insight that I was going to get pregnant once I started my mentorship program. I can't say I believed the intuition, but I most definitely felt it. So, when I say I was shocked, it was more so because what I was told in my spirit had come to fruition in the exact time frame that it was professed. I don't know about you but it's always a cool moment when God confirms His word to you. It invigorates and affirms your faith in ways that are undeniable.

It was time for a celebration. Who should I call? Everyone! Let's shout it on the mountain tops. "We are pregnant!" I quickly shot that down. It's way too early for a public service announcement, so I told myself to "shut that trap." Not a single word was to be spoken to anyone, not even a hint. Who'd think I'd have trouble holding my own secret. But I kept it mute.

For the next couple of weeks, I did what many first-timers do: took daily pictures of my belly, as if it grew by the day. It didn't. But the anticipation of my stomach stretching was a part of the thrilling experience. And you know what else I did? I started lathering my body early y'all. Dr. Oz mentioned moisturizing tips to minimize stretching—so I figured what better time to start than now. Let the *Google* searches on motherhood begin. The time had finally come.

God dropped a miracle on your girl and I was hype. Who wouldn't be? When your prayers are answered how do you feel? Happy? Relieved? Encouraged? It might depend on what you prayed for but for the most part, it is revitalizing. It goes back to the end of the scripture I mentioned in *Chapter Five*: *Hope deferred makes the heart sick, but when the desire comes, it is a tree of life*—it energizes and rejuvenates the soul (Proverbs 13:12). Especially, when that dream lands unexpectedly on what appears to be an irredeemable predicament.

The Passion Translation puts it simply: *When hope's dream seems to drag on and on, the delay can be depressing. But when at last your dream comes true, life's sweetness will satisfy your soul* (Proverbs 13:12 TPT).

It's a sweet feeling indeed. Perhaps, if the delay has been unimaginable—when the breakthrough arrives—it can seem too good to be true. At least for me it was, because behind this thrill was a bitter taste of pessimism. I attributed my cynical thoughts to my anxiousness to get through the first trimester. Since this was all new to me, it was imperative that I proceed with caution. I was also in the middle of producing a concert. I wanted no mishaps for me and the baby or the show.

Not Today, Satan!

With the showcase around the corner and the news of pregnancy, Lord knows I was in need of some tranquility. This was turning out to be a very stressful time. The workload was mounting and my tolerance level was at an all-time low.

Privy to the known factors of how anxiety can affect a pregnancy I was on guard and determined not to allow anyone to take me to TEN. No one told me that the best way to control raging hormones and emotional breakdowns was to avoid needy people at all costs, even if you considered them your friend.

Due to her life challenges, Ruby ultimately ghosted on promises she made as far as help for the showcase. With no return call, I was forced to cover these tasks, adding to my strain. A few days before the concert, my only priority was ensuring that my mentees had a successful showcase. Yet at the nth hour, Ruby called, hostile about having no ticket because we were at capacity. She had already harassed people under my purview before launching a full-scale diatribe about whether I like her or just tolerated her presence like a charity case.

I was not interested in pacifying a relationship or going back and forth with someone who was in need of friendship validation. Everything about this conversation took me back to the childish adolescent days of high school—college at the absolute latest. The reason this was bothersome for me is that this was a recurring episode with her. Time after time I felt myself having to affirm our friendship but *"Not Today Satan"* [colloquialism meaning today was not the day for it].

As a grown woman in my thirties, this type of conversation

had become foreign to me. I've had the same ride or die friends for over fifteen years. As far as I know, they are pretty secure in who they were, as well as in the solidity of our friendship, so we don't have these types of problems. Any offense we've ever had was usually brought to the surface, addressed, and we moved on like mature adults. But in this case, it took everything in me not to revisit my adolescent years and let Ruby HAVE IT!

Every word she spoke riled my spirit and my "nerve-ometer" was in a frenzy. My insides burned and my blood boiled, but believe it or not, I held my tongue. Nevertheless, I was disgusted by this whole situation that could have been avoided had she revealed that she was dealing with some insecurity issues at the top of the conversation instead of at the end. That's five thousand four hundred and fifty seconds of my life that I will never get back.

I know some of you are thinking, "Dacia! You sound a little insensitive." But like I said, my tolerance was low, and this was one of her overrated reruns. I recall her telling me years back that she didn't have any friends. And now I finally knew exactly why that statement held true.

I managed to get off the phone in peace explaining that it wasn't an appropriate time and that I would try to reach out after the showcase. Granted, the emphasis was on "try" because it was highly unlikely. I got off the phone and headed into rehearsal, trying my best to bury that conversation into the archives of *foolishness*, never to be revisited. Little did I know, that very conversation that took my blood pressure up would haunt me for weeks.

About fifteen minutes into rehearsal, I felt a rush of fluid drop from my body. I freaked, hauled butt out of the studio as discreetly as possible, and prayed to God that I was hallucinating—I wasn't! When I went to the restroom there was blood on my underwear. I panicked.

What is happening? My back hugged the bathroom wall and I called my husband in shambles.

"Calm down. Calm down. Everything is fine! Just try to relax and get through your rehearsal," he said.

RELAX! How can I possibly relax? My head was spinning out of control and I couldn't turn off the destructive sentiments assaulting my hope.

The goal was to keep my composure long enough to get through rehearsal. I didn't want to impose my personal fears onto my mentees. I locked in my poker face and walked out of the bathroom.

"Anybody got a tampon?" I yelled.

They were all in high school and college, so no one was moved by my candid outburst.

"No, but I got a pad!" one of them screamed back.

Ugh. A pad? (I assumed some of them hadn't graduated to the big leagues yet.) I absolutely hated pads, but desperate times called for desperate measures.

The anxieties and hypotheticals, though very present, were overshadowed by the busyness of my rehearsal day. So, the hours passed quickly. But when I got into the car, trepidation came crashing down like a ton of bricks. My ride home consisted of prayers and pleas to the heavens, hoping that God would pick up the Bat Phone and save me from the obscurities that rattled the foundations of my being.

9-1-1

When I got home, I pulled out my computer and headed straight to the online physician—*Google*. Like most, I presumed Google was my friend, so I attempted to self-diagnose based on the symptoms that I had seen. From the looks of it, this had the potential of being a few things—one of which I chose not to accept.

I must say that it was quite depressing reading oodles of stories that all ended badly. In an effort to lift my spirit, I rerouted the search engines and surfed the Christian sites that were saturated with miraculous testimonies of mothers who experienced complications such as mine yet prevailed with a child in their arms.

By the time I was done, the vast amount of information flowing from Google left me immensely disturbed. I left my office completely overwhelmed. I went into my room and collapsed on the bed. I stared at the pivoting ceiling fan in a pathetic attempt at hypnosis so I could fall into a deep sleep hoping to awaken from a terrible dream. My husband joined me in bed and stillness fell as he rested his hands on my stomach. I knew he was silently praying over my womb.

He fell asleep before me and once I heard his snore, I rolled over and headed back to the search engine on my cell phone. I looked up everything I could think of from miscarriages to how embryos look at seven weeks. Why? I don't know. Clearly, I wanted to torture myself further, knowing darn well we have to be cautious of what we see and hear right before bed to prevent a restless spirit. Instead, my preoccupied internet search allowed the spirit of fear to creep in that night, and my head was consumed with negative thoughts. I ended up having to pull out my Bible app and read scriptures until I fell asleep.

Against my better wishes, I slept with a pad on. According to my *Google* research, one of the sites strongly advised against the use of tampons until there was a clarification of what was causing the bleeding. At the crack of dawn, I was awakened by the need to pee and a slight bloat to the stomach. The restroom had not been my friend lately and I dreaded coming face to face with more blood. I sat in the dark on the toilet reluctant to turn the light on for fear of what it would expose. When I found the guts to hit the light switch, a pad saturated with blood greeted me. Every part of me wanted to fall out on the floor, ball up into the fetal position, and cry like a baby.

I woke up my husband and insisted that this was now an emergency and I needed to get to a doctor as soon as possible.

It was a Friday morning and we had just crossed the threshold of seven weeks after my LMP (last menstrual period). My first prenatal visit was scheduled for the following week but it was apparent that this could not wait. My husband and I tag-teamed on the mission of getting in to see a physician right away by calling every doctor's office in my immediate area, all of which were booked to the max with appointments for the day. It looked like I needed to prep for a visit to the dreadful ER.

I prayed for direction on whom to call and asked God for favor with someone who would see me today. Immediately, my spirit aroused and I felt this nudge to call Dr. Stone's office.

Now, you might be asking why I didn't call her first. Well, following her debut on *The Real Housewives,* I found it challenging to lock in an appointment that was anything less than three months out. I had defaulted to a local clinic for my annual exams while on the hunt for yet another gynecologist so I assumed a same-day appointment was absurd.

The unction to give Dr. Stone a call returned so I dialed her up in hopes of some supernatural favor only to hear, "I'm sorry, Mrs. Lewis, Dr. Stone doesn't have any availability today. *What's going on?"*

I was at my wit's end and on the verge of a breakdown. I gathered myself long enough to briefly explain to the receptionist the severity of what was happening. She must have heard the desperation in my voice. She abruptly interrupted my spill and requested to put me on hold.

"Please Jesus," I mumbled over the elevator music that serenaded my left ear.

"Mrs. Lewis?"

"Yes!"

"If you are okay with seeing our nurse practitioner, Ms. Reed, then we can fit you in at 9:00 A.M. Our ultrasound specialist is only here on Wednesdays, but Ms. Reed can do an exam and run some tests. Dr. Stone will peek in at the end of your visit to assess the problem."

"Yes, thank you! Thank you. I will be there at nine."

Chapter Eight
Wait It Out

God never sends your giant to kill you, He sends your giant to reveal you.

- Bishop T.D. Jakes

There was some solace in knowing that I was going to be seen by the doctor but I could still feel the angst of the unknown gnawing away at my optimism. Before heading into the exam room, I thought it wise to release the can. This time when I looked at my pad there were a few clots of blood and what looked like chunky pieces of tissue. Respiring deeply, I cleaned up and headed into the exam room.

In walked Ms. Reed, the nurse practitioner. She was a bit older than Dr. Stone and much more soft-spoken. Her spirit was gentle and motherly. After telling her what happened, she had her assistant draw blood to check my HCG (human chorionic gonadotropin) levels. HCG, according to the *American Pregnancy Association*[7], is often called the pregnancy hormone because it is made by cells formed in the placenta which nourish the egg after it has been fertilized and becomes attached to the uterine wall.

If HCG levels fall outside of what's considered a *normal range,* then doctors can conclude that you are pregnant. These levels can be detected in your bloodstream or urine; hence, we are able to confirm a pregnancy in the comfort of our own home by peeing on a stick.

As a woman progresses through her pregnancy, HCG levels should increase every two to three days as an embryo continues to develop. Any significant drop in those levels would indicate a possibility of complications.

Ms. Reed entered the room with the results.

"So … your HCG levels coincide with that of a pregnancy," she said. "At this point, we can only go by your levels; therefore, I cannot confirm that this is a threat of a miscarriage."

In a nutshell, she said: You're pregnant. You're bleeding. We don't know why (yet).

A creek of the door followed a knock, and in waltzed a sympathetic Dr. Stone.

"How are you, sweetheart?"

"EGH!" I grumbled.

"I know, I know. Let me take a look." While she was probing my vagina, she reiterated the information explained earlier by Ms. Reed. When she wrapped up her exam she asked, "Have you felt anything drop from you?"

Drop from me? I had no clue what she was talking about and I didn't want to know either.

"Ugh! No, not that I know of, just blood with what looks like clots," I said, referring to the continual spew from my body.

Dr. Stone nodded with no further enlightenment on her question. Her pen scrolled volumes on my chart. She handed it to Ms. Reed.

"I will see you first thing Monday morning," Dr. Stone said. "We will do another exam and check your levels again. And on Wednesday we will do an ultrasound. If you are pregnant, your numbers will significantly increase within the next 72 hours and if there is a dilemma, they will begin to move in the opposite direction."

I gave her a nod as Dr. Stone exited the room. Ms. Reed scheduled an ultrasound for the following Wednesday and gave me a precautionary warning urging me to take it easy. I already had ants in my pants, and now they wanted me to wait it out for five more days in ambivalence.

Seriously, God?

Ms. Reed must have read the look of concern on my face. "Go home and put your feet up," she said, tapping me on the leg. "Pray and try not to worry!"

I left this appointment feeling just as bleak as when I arrived. The ride home was awkward, partly because I was in a silent daze. And then there's this super pad with wings they gave me to put on after the exam that went from my belly button to my lower back. *Man, I hate pads.*

WHAM!

With all this blood departing from my body, I was in the mood for a nice juicy Angus beef burger to calm the raging monster on the inside of me; so, we stopped at one of my favorite burger joints near our old apartment. The food was amazing; nothing to soothe a good mope like a burger and fries. Well satisfied, the "itis" kicked in quickly [itis: an African American colloquialism for food coma resulting in drowsiness after a meal]. I couldn't wait to crawl into bed and shed all of my built-up tears until my eyes were too heavy to stay open. Thinking was too toilsome at the moment, so I stared out of the window gazing at nature, watching the cars go by.

WHAM! A jolt of pain blindsided me like a hit from a linebacker, causing me to grab hold of the door handle.

WHAM! Another one hit right in the lower belly. Each sharp pain came in waves and my anticipation for the next caused me to clinch the door with one hand and my husband's arm with the other.

My breathing intensified as I yelled out an aching moan with each spasm.

My husband instantly went into prayer mode trying his best to reassure me that we were almost home. The excruciating discomfort made a ten-minute ride feel like hours. If this was anything like being in labor, then I wanted no parts of it.

I yelled for God to stop the pain, but His ear must have been too far off to hear me because the pain did not stop and neither did the burden of speculating that this was a miscarriage.

After pushing through the agonizing car ride, I ran into the house and slumped down on the toilet hoping a good bowel movement would fix this problem. I hadn't eaten beef in a while, so my hope was that this was just my upset stomach rejecting the greasy burger that I had just devoured. Thankfully, I let a good one out and the cramps diminished.

"Thank You, Lord!" I rejoiced, choosing to believe that it was just the burger.

I was worn out from the adventures of the day. I knocked down a couple of Tylenol and got in the bed. Before taking a nap, I grabbed my journal to document the events of the day and have a few words with God.

Journal Entry #18

Today was horrible. Where were You? It felt as if You weren't there when I was going through one of the scariest moments of my life. My spirit is distraught at the possibility of what this could be. Honestly, I just want it to be over. If this is what it looks like, then let's get this over with so I can grieve and move on with my life.

I mustered up the strength to get out of the bed and draw some bathwater. I even added some bubbles and lit a candle to tranquilize my spirit. I put on some Christian music, turned on the water jets and relaxed, meditating on the words of each song that shuffled through my playlist. My bleeding came to a halt and I was able to maneuver pain-free throughout the rest of the day.

I texted my demon-slaying prayer warriors and alerted them to send one up for me. They know I can hold my own at the throne so if I am asking for prayer, then it must be serious. I didn't disclose too much information so they didn't know what they were praying for, but I knew the Lord would reveal to them exactly how to pray.

All of a sudden, I felt this unusual peace in my spirit. I was reminded of the name Immanuel—God is with us. A scripture came to mind reassuring me of His presence:

So do not fear, for I am with you; do not be dismayed, for I am your God. I will strengthen you and help you; I will uphold you with My righteous right hand.

Isaiah 41:10 NIV

No matter what was happening God was with me. I went to bed feeling good that night. My prayer warriors had hit the frontline covering me, the bleeding had completely stopped and I was feeling hopeful that this pregnancy would make it through the storm. I put on another super pad—just in case—hit the lights, said my prayers, and turned in for the night.

BLOOP!

Rise and Shine. The sun peeped through the blinds introducing me to Saturday morning, a day of rest. I glanced over and saw my husband was still knocked out, exhausted from the previous day's shenanigans. I quietly rolled out of bed to avoid disturbing him.

I went to the restroom per usual early morning release with little concern since the bleeding had ceased after I had taken a bath the previous night. I pulled down my undergarments and the super pad was filled to the max. I rolled my eyes, let out a groan, and plopped down on the toilet to pee. As soon as I sat down, I heard a *bloop* noise like something dropped in the toilet.

"What the hell is that?" I thought.

"Ok, I know this isn't the vestige of a bowel movement because I barely even sat down on the toilet!" Suddenly, I flashed back to when Dr. Stone asked me if anything had dropped from me which alerted me that this was not good. I froze for a moment and contemplated my next move.

Do I flush?

Do I look?

Do I get it?

Understandably, some might be completely grossed out by the next part of the story but for those that can bear it, let's go!

I graduated from college with a minor in biology, and my inquiring mind wanted to know; therefore, I dunked my hand in the water and got the mysterious circular object out of the toilet. The decision I had to make was whether or not I was about to dissect the sac that I just pulled out of the toilet. Remember, the Curious George in me had already Googled what embryos look like around this stage of the pregnancy.

I flopped back down on the toilet, wrapped the bizarre thingamajig in tissue and mentally prepared myself for what I was about to do. I prayed to God asking Him to give me the gall to be able to handle whatever it was that I was about to dismember. And, if what I was about to see ended up being what I thought, I prayed God would comfort me and heal my heart from what might be one of the most devastating moments of my life.

I took a deep breath, tore the sac open, and . . .

WHEW!

EMPTY! Whew! A wave of relief came over me. All I saw was what looked like blood clots attached to the inner lining of this sac. It didn't resemble anything like what I thought an eight-week embryo should look like based on my web-surfing.

I must have alarmed my husband with my lengthy stay in the bathroom. "You okay in there?" he called out from the bedroom.

"No, we need to call Dr. Stone. Something dropped out of my vagina."

By this time, I had wrapped the doohickey in toilet tissue and laid it on my bathroom counter. I called Dr. Stone's emergency line since it was the weekend. The operator said she would page her and expect Dr. Stone to give me a call within the hour. She called three minutes later.

"Hey Mrs. Lewis, what's going on?" Dr. Stone asked.

"Hey Dr. Stone. I had something drop from me this morning when I went to use the restroom."

"Okay, what did it look like?"

I tried to explain to her what I saw, but it was hard to describe, so I just called it "a ball of tissue." And guess what her next question was? Take one guess? You guessed it.

"Did you happen to get it out of the toilet?"

"Yup, I sure did," I said.

There was no shame in my game. I wanted to know what this was and the only way to find that out was to take it to the lab.

"Good! You are a brave girl," she continued. "Most people would not have fetched it, but I am so glad that you did. Okay, where is it now?"

"It's wrapped up in a piece of toilet tissue lying on my bathroom counter."

"This might seem gross, but I need you to put it in the refrigerator."

"Excuse me?"

"No, I mean take it, wrap it in a paper towel, place it in a Ziplock plastic bag, put it in the fridge, and bring it with you on Monday."

"Okay, will do," I said. "But what is it?"

"We won't know until we examine it. Based upon your description it might be a gestational sac that has passed through. I will see you on Monday. Try to relax and do something to take your mind off of it."

I said to myself, "If one more person tells me to relax, I am going to scream. A ball of confusion just fell out of my vagina. My whole body is confused, and my pregnancy looks to be in jeopardy. Relaxing is not an option—easier said than done."

Ignorant of how this all works, I decided to run to the 'ole dollar store and pick up a pregnancy test.

Well, to be honest, I picked up five of them. Deep down I wanted to believe that this was just tissue passing and it hadn't affected my BFP.

When I got home, I lined the tests up across the tub, peed

on the sticks and waited. My HCG levels were still showing I was pregnant.

All five were positive.

Chapter Nine
Wait and See

True rest is being still and knowing that God is God—no matter what is happening around us.

-Stormie Omartian

M y early appointment on Monday morning came pretty quickly. I carried the bag with the mystery tissue in the side pocket of my purse. It was a rather quick office visit, as I was only there to get my blood drawn and drop the specimen to the lab specialist. I handed her the bag and she looked at me like I was crazy. "What is this?" she asked. I guess they didn't give her the memo.

She warily examined the bag from afar as I ran down a quick synopsis of what happened. Amid telling the story, her eyes lit up with great anticipation for what further tests would reveal. She was like a kid in the candy store, as this clearly tickled her fancy.

"Great!" she said, grabbing the bag from my hand, her eyeballs working all angles as if to borough through the paper towel.

"This stuff doesn't faze you?" I asked.

"No. I love doing things like this," she said. "You wouldn't believe some of the things people bring in here that I get to play with. This is nothing! I'm glad you got it out of the toilet because now we can run tests and know exactly what this is." *(See, I did the right thing. If something ever drops out of you and you don't know what it is, put on your bold boots, grab it out of the toilet, and bring it in for testing.)*

They drew blood again to check my HCG levels and I briefly spoke with Ms. Reed.

"Mrs. Lewis I will give you a call with the results of your blood test before your ultrasound appointment. If the levels drop this would coincide with the evidence of a miscarriage." She ended the appointment with encouragement. "But we still don't know. Keep praying, doll. We will see you Wednesday."

Still, no definitive answer. This was turning into a week from hell and it was only Monday. But, surely the ultrasound specialist would clear up the chaos and this baptism of fire would be over after Wednesday's appointment—good or bad.

I think my intuition kicked in and I had become acquiescent to having a miscarriage. My flesh was unsettled judging by my constant fiddling of things, but my spirit was at peace. I prayed, in case there was a whim of a chance that God was going to pull through with a miracle.

Journal Entry #19

I am trying not to be angry but I am. I'm weak and emotionally drained.

Your Word says that You will not put more on me than I can bear, and a miscarriage is more than I can bear at the moment. Everything that I see tells me that this is not good, so how can this come from You when You are not a cruel God?

After I dropped off the specimen to the lab I sat with my husband on the couch and vented about our adversities. He was convinced that God was still in the miracle-working business, and we were still pregnant. I mean the man's faith had gone through the roof. If he was at all moved by our circumstances, he didn't show a lick of uncertainty. He was in it to win it. He prayed and praised, thanking God for the miraculous.

He looked me dead in the eye and said, "I don't believe God would show us a glimpse of a miracle only to strip it away. He would not bring me out into the deep and let me drown. That is not the God that I serve. The tests still say you are pregnant and that is the only word I have to go on. So, at this moment, while we wait and see, I am choosing to believe in God and put His word to the test until He says otherwise."

When I look back on it, I think he had to be strong because I was debilitated mentally, physically, emotionally and spiritually. I had nothing more to give. My inner being was shot, so all I could muster up was, "Lord, I believe; please help my unbelief" (Mark 9:24), a scripture that I had tucked away in my heart for rainy days like these. My hope was that God would honor that simple prayer. My journal again became the safe haven where I poured my heart out to God and articulated the words that I could not verbally express.

Journal Entry #20

Based upon what I have seen thus far, it's hard to believe that You would allow this. I've seen and read of miracles far greater than the one I am asking for. So, I shall not be moved because nothing is impossible with or for You.

There I was, crying myself to sleep trying to gather faith the size of a mustard seed. My heart ached at the thought of a miscarriage so I tried to focus on His love, His grace, and His comfort. But none of it seemed present during this downpour of distress.

False Positive

Ms. Reed called Tuesday afternoon with the news that my HCG levels had significantly dropped. The ultrasound was still on for Wednesday and after hanging up the phone I had come to terms with what was happening and could offer no more hope of a different outcome.

I came into the doctor's office on Wednesday with a, "Let's do this so I can get on with my life" attitude. I undressed, lay on the exam table, and turned to my husband who was sitting in the chair next to me rocking back and forth with his hands in his lap. I offered a *ho-hum* smile knowing he was over there still praying for a miracle.

The specialist came in and got straight to work. When the cold gel hit my belly, my nonchalant front was immediately exposed. My nerves kicked into high gear and I could feel my heart pounding. There was this tiny ray of hope for a supernatural miracle, but it was buried so deep with pessimism that it was impossible to clench.

I waited to hear the inevitable.

She scanned the transducer across my stomach leaning into the monitor with a look of confusion.

"Hmm, I still see something that resembles a sac."

I saw my husband's eyes light up at her intel, but I was deadpanned and unmoved.

Careful not to make any assumptions, either way, the specialist ordered the assistant to get Dr. Stone. Soon after, she scrammed out of the door as if she didn't trust the assistant to deliver the message properly. I turned toward my husband.

"What is going on?"

"This is it," my husband (with his adorable self) said. "I believe there is another sac with a baby. This is the miracle we've been praying for."

"I want this to be over," I said, blasé in tone. "Either we are pregnant or we aren't. I just want off this roller coaster ride. It ain't fun. At all!"

As Dr. Stone rushed into the room, everyone else behind her, she gave me a quick, "Hey hun. How are you doing?" and instantaneously took the transducer and started inspecting my insides. This was turning into an episode of ER.

"Mm-hmm ... okay! It appears there is still some debris in the uterus!"

There was no additional sac and there was no heartbeat. What the specialist saw on the monitor was excess tissue that needed to pass which confirmed that this was an abnormal pregnancy that was self-aborting.

"More bleeding?" was all I could think about. "What kind of month-long-period? Thanks, but no thanks!" I deflected my thoughts to the inconvenience of an extended period, instead of the fact that what I feared was actually happening.

I didn't want to face the facts. I wanted to forget about them. But when I saw the last bit of hope that my husband was gripping on for dear life get trampled over by the news, I knew this would not be easily forgotten. My heart went out to him as I watched his spirit crush with every word Dr. Stone spoke.

"What's next?" I asked.

"I recommend scheduling you for a D&C procedure this Friday," she said.

"And what exactly does that do?"

"A D&C is a procedure to rid your uterus of all the debris caused by the pregnancy aborting."

"And that's it?"

"That's it dear. I know it's been a hectic ride." Dr. Stone said.

"Hectic is an understatement."

Reality had not just set in; it smacked us right in the face. The ride home was silent. I saw the anger in my husband's eyes. He was boiling and I didn't know what to say or how to soothe his pain. I asked how he was doing and he said nothing.

When we got to the house, he sat beside me while we waited for the other to speak. He laid his head on my shoulder and burst into tears. I can count on half of one hand how many times I have seen my husband cry. And that's with me calling a watered eye crying. So, by far, seeing him bawl was unnerving.

At least my husband never let his faith waiver. He took God at His word right up until the last moment—when the doctor confirmed that we were no longer pregnant. He was a trooper, my rock who held me down. He believed for me when I could no longer believe for myself. If anyone deserved the gold medal of faith, it was him. He had passed the faith test right up to the very end. And now here he was, heartsick and in despair, feeling as if God had left us high and dry.

"Why did this have to happen to us?" he asked.

I had the same question. Why did this happen? And how did this happen?

A flashback bolted through my head—RUBY!!! Suddenly every ounce of grace that I extended to her at the end of our conversation was null and void. It was now replaced with fury as I blamed her petty behavior for what we now knew was a miscarriage. Ruby, during what I'm sure was a mid-life crisis, was simply doing what she does at the wrong time and I simply didn't have the wherewithal to shut it down sooner.

Seeing the gravity of my husband's pain instantly led me to even more questions: Did this situation with Ruby cause more stress than my body could take? Was my inability to entertain her nonsense detrimental to my child? Would everything have worked out fine with this pregnancy without that heightened moment of aggravation? Was it a pile-up of stress, on which Ruby was just the final straw? Ultimately, I didn't know whether the remnants of that futile conversation were the cause of my miscarriage.

The truth is, I had no idea how to calibrate the degree to which my emotional discomfort might inhibit my pregnancy. But I desperately needed a reason, a tangible reason on how this came to pass. Even if there was no obvious responsible party, I found it easier to blame Ruby than to reject my faith, again. So, for now, TAG! Ruby was it!

Good News or Bad News

Initially, when we received our BFP we were debating on when we would tell our parents. Just so happened that our moms were coming into town later that evening to help me prepare for my mentee's showcase. This would be the perfect time to share the good news. Only the good news was now the bad news.

We deemed it necessary to do damage control before they arrived to avoid an influx of sentiments upon arrival. I couldn't handle that. There were too many untouched emotions that I could not express. I am not a public *sobber*, so I didn't want anyone tugging on my heartstrings with their tears of sympathy.

I called my mom first, gave her the cliff notes version of the mayhem and she gave me a jarring response. She was enthused which left me borderline confused.

"This is good news," she said. "This is a sign that it will happen. You can get pregnant and you will get pregnant, so don't lose hope! Rejoice I say, rejoice."

Interesting take on the matter at hand, but her chipper outlook barely pacified the avalanche of sadness that was cached for a later time. Helpful? Maybe. But I couldn't see mountaintop vistas at that moment. I didn't want to hear anything about future TTC or pregnancies on the horizon. I was numb and nothing swayed me either way so everyone could keep their optimism for another day.

Although it had been a tumultuous morning, to say the least, this train was still trucking. My husband was headed to pick up our moms from the airport and I was holding a rehearsal on my living room floor. I had already prepared myself for their emotional entrance just in case there was a somber mood or breakdown when they first saw me.

When they got to the house, my mom ran to hug me, a beaming smile on her face. My mother-in-law offered a puppy dog face with a dismal "Awww!" patting my back as she hugged me. I shielded myself from any unanticipated emotional releases and quickly disengaged from her hug. I didn't need any help being sad, so I gave her a stoic "it's all good" look and went right back to rehearsals.

Was I good? I don't know, but the showcase aided me in corseting my raw emotions. I didn't have time to grieve. I was producing a concert and my big girl panties were strapped on tight. No time for pity parties, especially if such parties were initiated by someone other than me, the beneficiary of all this absurdity.

The next day I slept in and prepared myself for the D&C that was happening the following day. I avoided any conversation with the moms about the calamity. When they asked how I was doing, I said good and pivoted the conversation. My mentees had been preparing for this day for almost a year so all feelings were subdued to the back of the mind. I wasn't going to let this or anything else stop me from producing the best show possible for them.

To this day, my mentees are unaware of what I was going through the weeks leading up to their show. I didn't think it was fair to put that on them. By no means did I want them to freak out, take any sort of blame for all the stress, or above all, feel sorry for me. I hate pity.

Chapter Ten
Waiting To Exhale

When we choose thankful prayer over wallowing in anxiety and worry, we are demonstrating an unwavering faith in God.

-Priscilla Shirer

Friday morning rolled around quickly. It was two days before the showcase, and all was halted for *doomsday*. Today was my D&C procedure. The moms tagged along for support. The night before, my mom was the first to ask, "Do you want me to go with you?"

"I don't care!" I said. Next thing I know Friday morning rolled around and everyone was in the car headed with me to the hospital. I wish I could say I felt loved at the time, but my focus was getting through this ordeal and back to my order of business.

I popped in the muscle relaxer and painkiller that Dr. Stone prescribed to help with the discomfort of the procedure. I slouched into the hospital bed and scanned the room as I prepared for the final moments of a bad dream. I was on edge, not fully comprehending what was about to happen, so my husband joined me in the exam room to help alleviate the anxiety. He would be my reinforcement in case I got the urge to run for the hills during their rigmarole. I was also feeling the relaxation from the meds and wanted a coherent witness at my side.

After hearing all the information and signing my life away, my husband was escorted out of the room so that Dr. Stone could proceed. He gave me a nod of reassurance and exited. It was time.

Lights Out

For those unfamiliar, a D&C, also known as dilation and curettage, is a surgical procedure performed after a first-trimester miscarriage. As stated by the *American Pregnancy Association*[8], dilation refers to the opening of the cervix; curettage refers to removing the contents in the uterus. Curettage is performed by scraping the uterine wall with a curette instrument or by a suction curettage (also called vacuum aspiration).

Dr. Stone forewarned me that the blasting sound of the machine makes the process seem scarier than what it actually is. I closed my eyes and said a quick prayer to calm my nerves. She clicked that sucker on and I heard what sounded like a lawnmower ready to plow me over. She was right; the noise was most disturbing.

The machine resembled a vacuum with a long suction tube at the end. When I say long, I mean long, but thank God it was only a few centimeters in width, no wider than a straw. It was more uncomfortable and loud than it was painful. I watched as her arms started working—her gloves full of blood as she scraped the lining of my uterus, sucking out whatever debris was left in me. I shut my eyes, wanting to keep them closed the entire time. But my *Curious George* was aroused, and my eyes became fixated on the clear tube that was attached to the suction. I needed to see what came out.

I watched as the blood seeped through the tube traveling into the machine with what looked like chunks of meat within the red fluid. Once I saw the first wad of tissue, a wave of emotions swarmed my body. A few tears dropped from my eyes. I quickly turned my head to the side and wiped them away to avoid attention. Any anticipation of this turning out to be a different outcome ended at that moment. IT. WAS. OVER.

If someone asked me what happened, I would have told them in my uneducated opinion, R-U-B-Y is what happened. Don't mistake it, what she did was out of line. But in my desperate attempt to make sense of what happened, I kept landing on her and how she selfishly would not quit. I figured I'd ask Dr. Stone for some insight on how this miscarriage could have happened.

"Dr. Stone? Quick question. Do you think this was due to stress because I really lost my cool the day I started bleeding?"

She explained that there are a number of factors that can attribute to a miscarriage. And went on to say, "Mrs. Lewis, I believe our ancestors had to endure immeasurably more pain and suffering than we experience today and they were still able to give birth. So personally, I don't think a trivial amount of stress would have caused this miscarriage. The great thing about the body is that it can immediately recognize abnormalities and self-abort. Although heartbreaking and sometimes unbearable to fathom, it's actually pretty extraordinary that our bodies are that intelligent."

Thanks to Dr. Stone, Ruby was off the hook. I guess no matter how hard you try to make sense of tragedy, some things are just unexplainable.

I walked out of the doctor's office with a stiff upper lip and hopped back into the swing of things refusing to relay any signs of weakness to the moms or the mentees. The show went on without a glitch. Every performer killed the stage. I was a proud mama.

And the Academy Award goes to ...

Yes, clearly I had won the award for best actress. No one would've ever guessed that as I stood on that stage thanking our audience and bowing to roaring applause that my body was ridding itself of the remnants of a miscarriage. A noteworthy performance.

And ... Scene. Lights Out.

The Walking Dead

The raucous ceased, mothers were gone, and the emotions left unturned rose to the surface while I was home alone with nothing but time on my hands. The affliction of a lost pregnancy had anesthetized my mind and I was walking dead; active and coherent but lifeless on the inside. The thought of trying again was non-existent.

I was somewhat grateful for the doctor's order not to have intercourse for a month. I wasn't in the mood and I sure as hell wasn't ready to try again or hear, "keep trying, it will happen" from anyone.

All I wanted was to be left alone, by everyone, including my husband.

He bounced back pretty quickly. After that moment of brokenness on the couch, it was as if God dialed his personal cell phone and spoke a word that resuscitated him.

My husband regarded the whole ordeal as a test of faith and started walking the trail to optimism. More like running, and he wasn't the only one. My mom and my best friends were on this chipper trail with him.

Everyone seemed to have on the rose-colored glasses. In a way, it annoyed me. All the "cheer up" and "hop back on the horse" talk warranted a corresponding fake smile and eye roll. This was easier said than done, people. Not a single one of them had experienced this before; so, how could they tell me to hope again—and so quickly?

"Look, I know you don't want to hear this, but this is a good sign!" one of my friends chomped. "You will get pregnant and that is what we are going to believe—period. So, you're pregnant and I will keep declaring it until it manifests."

"From your mouth to God's ears," I said. "I have nothing to say."

Well, at least not aloud.

Journal Entry #21

I just don't get it. What was the purpose of this? Maybe if I knew why it happened I could cope and move on. What did we do to deserve this, to wait so long for this glimpse of hope for You to tease us and take it away? That's like giving a baby a piece of candy, letting them lick it to see how good it tastes only for You to snatch it back and say—just kidding you can't have it. Why would You allow our hope to be crushed with such a massive blow? I am trying to make sense of all this ... but I can't.

Although I didn't have the unction to get up and pray, I found myself in my same routine: walking upstairs to my office every morning with my journal in hand. For the next few weeks my mornings consisted of sitting quietly in my prayer closet with my pen saying everything my mouth couldn't manage to utter:

Journal Entry #22

I am hurt but I am here. I have nothing to give but I am here. I am tempted to give up on You once again, but I find myself here anyway hoping that You will honor what little I have to offer.

I played worship music while I wrote, and it turned into communion as I rocked back and forth to the songs that spoke to my spirit, tears long held inside streaming down my face. I was releasing the pain without mumbling a single word.

Journal Entry #23

Look God! Let me be honest with You. I am pissed. I am embarrassed. I am bitter. I am numb. I am speechless. How do You expect me to keep the faith when my heart aches so much? I feel like I'm trapped in a cage of disappointment, wallowing in agony. I'm at a crossroads once again. And I ain't going to lie, giving up seems much easier right now than trusting that this will get better. Just saying.

Eventually, I started reading back what I had written in my entries, vocalizing what lay on each page. As I listened to myself quote my own words, I could see that despair was summoning me for another round of beating. My goal was not to allow my aching heart to take me through another cycle of unbelief and agnosticism. This time there would be no disconnecting from God.

Like clockwork, daily I went to God. I can't say my prayers were long or my worship intense. I just did what I could out of what I had left in the reserve tank and I relied on God to supply the rest. My prayer was that He would heal my broken heart and crucify the things that were overwhelming me. Instead of airing my grievances to God, closing my journal, and walking out of my prayer closet just as depleted and hopeless as when I walked in, I made a decision to speak the promises of God over my life.

Let me clarify, I still complained and asked a whole lot of questions, some of which, I am still waiting for Him to answer. But I closed each entry with a confession of faith, "God You are faithful, and You have never failed me yet."

Journal Entry #24

Heal my heart, God! I know that You are faithful and that You heal the broken-hearted. Give me peace and most of all, help me to hope again.

I'm not sure if most women would be able to shake such a tragedy, but I know choosing to go to God every day in spite of how I felt was the quintessential key to my stability. There was something about going before God with a sincere heart. I always walked out with what I needed to get me through the day—a sense of serenity. I imagine this was the "peace of God, which surpasses all understanding" that the Bible references in

Philippians 4:7. Not only was I healing physically from the procedure, but the time I spent with God was mending my heart and deepening my trust in Him.

Chapter Eleven
The WAITer

When you carry the WEIGHT of yesterday, it will ruin the POWER of today and the PROGRESS of tomorrow.

-Dr. Tony Evans

T wo months later. My husband had the day off, not by choice, but because he worked until the wee hours of the morning. I insisted he stay home from work and catch up on some much-needed rest; since it was a beautiful day outside, he complied.

We decided to take a stroll in the park and grab some lunch. I—being an "if it ain't broke don't fix it" kind of chick—like to stick to my favorite restaurants because they deliver a satisfying experience every time. I had a taste for some southern cuisine at the spot around the corner from our house but my husband, being the spontaneous one, recommended we try a new spot.

A soul food restaurant a few blocks from where we walked popped up on his phone's search engine and he proposed we venture down the street. I acknowledged his proposal but wasn't a bit interested. I casually browsed the menus of the local restaurants as we strolled the streets of downtown and avoided giving him an answer. I came across a menu in the window of a restaurant we hadn't tried and decided that this might be suitable for both of us.

When it came time to place our order, the waiter had a rebuttal to everything that I wanted from the menu. Their lunch hour had just passed, and all of the signature goodies were depleted.

What are the odds that all four entrees that piqued my interest were no longer available? A complete bust!

Well, that was my cue to vacate the premises. By now it was approaching 3 p.m. and I was getting hangry [on the verge of anger due to lack of food]. I looked at the surrounding restaurants and, in disapproval, I finally relented and chose the food place that my husband originally mentioned.

"Are you sure?" My husband asked.

"Yes!" I said, not really sure as much as I was hungry.

Mother Teresa

My husband pitched its greatness on the ride over by expressing it has high ratings online. The reviews raved about the atmosphere with the main attraction being Ms. Teresa. We walked in and were greeted by a resounding, "Hey babies! Come on in and sit wherever you'd like." It was none other than … Ms. Teresa. Her pictures decked the wall identifying her as the visionary of the joint. Certainly, the masses flocked to this place just to get a piece of Ms. Teresa.

Everything on the menu made me leap for joy. It had been a while since I had some good old-fashioned southern food that made me feel like I was back home in Texas. Her homemade secrets had to be the reason this place was the talk of the town. When we got our food, my mouth salivated at the mac n' cheese that adorned my plate. It looked just like grandma used to make it—a little toasted at the top and definitely not made with powdered cheese. We laughed and joked as we enjoyed the delightfulness on our plates. The food was delicious. This was turning into a great mid-day date.

When I looked up to take in the atmosphere, I noticed a huge Bible that was open on the counter where Ms. Teresa was seated. I told my husband, "Ms. Teresa over there in that Good Book, getting that Word." We chuckled, but as we continued to eat, I heard the murmuring of prayer in my left ear. I subtly glanced over and saw Ms. Teresa praying hand-in-hand with a customer.

"Wow! She ain't playing," I told my husband.

The reviews were right. There was something about Ms. Teresa. Her spirit felt familiar. She reminded my husband and me of the matriarchs of our family, our grandmothers. Both of them are praying women, gracious, and giving; but with a mean stare that made you get in line as a kid. Yes, that was Ms. Teresa!

My husband took to her well as she checked in on our table

frequently. When we got up to leave, she asked how we liked the food and flawlessly segued to, "Do you have any kids?"

"Not yet," we answered in unison. We learned this was the best way to answer this uninvited question. It enabled us to speak in faith what we were believing God to accomplish without engaging the inquisitive.

Ms. Teresa persisted, "Are you ready to have kids?"

I hesitated with a hunch of what was to come, but my husband was prompt.

"Yes!" he said.

"Well, come here!" she urged.

I must have been in a trance because before I knew it my feet stepped in Ms. Teresa's direction. This was a clear violation of my *Rules of Engagement*. There is absolutely no way that I would ever allow a complete stranger to blatantly invade my privacy, nor would I ever yield to her summon after intruding into my personal life. Everything about this went against my precepts, but my heart moved closer and closer to her direction as if she had something I was in need of.

"Sit right here and you right there," she directed, indicating the seat next to her for me and the one on my opposite side for my husband. She told him to grab my right hand as she laid her hand on my stomach and began to pray.

My eyes started to water at the initial beckoning of her call so by this time I was in full-blown waterworks.

She prayed with the utmost intensity as she grabbed a hold of my stomach and pressed in harder and harder with each commanding word. I wept uncontrollably refusing to look up because I didn't want to acknowledge the bystanders who might've taken notice of the ruckus. She went on to speak in her heavenly language and declared conception to "come to pass" in the name of Jesus. I shut my eyes tighter and concentrated on receiving the words, struggling to block out what felt like shame and judgment from potential onlookers.

She interrupted her prayer and asked me if I believed. I said, "yes," with no hesitation, even though that was my quandary. She continued in her prayer, acknowledging my yes as an indicator to press deeper into prayer.

"May it be unto me according to Your Word, God," I said faintly under my breath. "Lord I believe. Please, please help my unbelief."

I received every word she spoke, partly in faith and partly in desperation for some type of sign from God. It had been a rough summer. Two months had passed since the miscarriage took place and I was still recouping from the blow. Any edification that encouraged and helped me to cling to my faith was now well received and embraced as a confirmation that God was in this thing with me.

As she came to a close in "Jesus' name" she looked me

square in the eye and said, "This will happen, you hear me! I want you to come back and visit me once you find out you are pregnant."

"I sure will." I confidently said.

Ms. Teresa opened her arms to give me a big hug. She hugged both of us and said she loved us. My natural thought was this woman doesn't even know us, but I knew what she meant. It was love. It was the love of Christ and we proclaimed our love back to her.

I turned around, reluctant to lift my head to avoid making eye contact with spectators. As we walked out, she said, "Now go get busy!" We laughed along with the audience in the restaurant who cheered. They were well aware of what had transpired although I hoped they were too busy enjoying their food. But it was welcomed; they were in agreement, joining their faith with ours and rooting us on.

The Manna House

We sat in the car for a moment and marveled at the events of the day as tears fell from my eyes. From the initial indecisiveness of what I wanted to eat, to the restaurant that ran out of everything I wanted to order, to *hangrily* deciding to go back to the place my husband first suggested; this was one for the books. Coincidence? I'd say not. God makes no mistakes.

This was a divine appointment.

As we drove off from the parking lot, I found myself staring at the marquee with the restaurant's name on it: The Manna House. You see, my husband never mentioned the name of the restaurant but as soon as I saw it the revelation of God hit me like a ton of bricks. Manna means bread from heaven. The miraculous food that fell from the sky (out of nowhere) that God provided to the Israelites while they were in the wilderness (Exodus 16). Manna was a miracle blessing that required total dependence and trust in God's provision.

A wealth of emotions came over me. I was full, literally and spiritually. There was this massive sensation residing in my chest yearning to be released as I put it all together. God had provided me with manna—a prophetic word/food from heaven—that would sustain me for the journey ahead. It required that I depend completely on Him and trust His timing because Ms. Teresa didn't say when or how it would happen, she just said, "It will happen, just BELIEVE. You have to BELIEVE."

My faith got a shot of a 5-hour energy drink from encountering Ms. Teresa and a shift was made. I could feel my faith rising to the occasion and I joined my husband on the trail to optimism. All of my past disappointments were just that, in the past. God had not forgotten about me. In fact, He sent me to The Manna House to confirm that He has heard every single prayer cried out in my *secret place*. God renewed my hope that day and revealed Himself to me in a big way.

I believe God sent me an angel that day to reassure me of things to come. There was no way that she would have known our circumstance; she was led by the Holy Spirit to speak life into our situation. It was the food (the Word) that I needed to hold me up while I fought this fight of faith. Ms. Teresa heard from God and gave me a prophetic word straight from the heavens. This was a ray of sunshine that I had been praying for, my affirmation that God was listening. I believed God's Word. I received God's Word and I made a choice that day to hold on to God's word, no matter what came up against me.

God was asking me to release the weight of unanswered questions and trust His plan. Not just with regards to conception, but in all things, because He is faithful.

Journal Entry #25

All I can say is … Thank You! Thank You Lord, for a divine appointment with my very own Mother Teresa. Grateful!

Worth The Weight

Life is a continuous roller coaster of highs and lows. Peaks and valleys are synonymous. We can't have one without the other. Although we tend to define life by monumental milestones, the truth is we live most of our lives in the in-between. The problem in our contemporary culture is that we savor our mountaintop experiences which leave us yearning for the next big breakthrough, forgetting that it's impossible to move from mountain to mountain without experiencing a hike through the valley (the in-between). Without a quantum leap to forfeit the *in-between* journey, we are forced to wait it out.

It is during these waiting periods that you may face moments where you are tempted to question if God even cares. Everything you believed about Him for years could hang in the balance as you wait with an insurmountable weight resting on you. You may also begin to question God's existence. But know that every roadblock in front of you or curveball thrown at you is an opportunity to get closer to God. The pressures of life will either push you to pray or push you astray.

I don't know anyone who thinks waiting seasons are fun, but they do provide opportunities for growth and development. Active waiting is the training ground for maturity in Christ. God uses these times of adversity to work in our hearts and develop our character. Always remember, your waiting season is never a wasted season.

Disappointments are inevitable and recovery time is specific to each person. My recovery wasn't as swift as my husband's, but I got there. I think I struggled because God has always been good to me and this weight of waiting was a complete contradiction of what our relationship had been like. But I eventually recovered and crossed the finish line and my relationship with God is so much stronger.

To this day, I am still choosing to walk by faith and not by sight (2 Corinthians 5:7). Now I have to be honest, sometimes my faith isn't mountain-moving faith, sometimes it's barely mustard seed faith, but I still choose faith as I wait. Waiting is not always easy, but waiting stretches your faith and faith is one of the vital components that turns our trials into triumphs and our tests into testimonies. You may not know when you'll win, but one thing I know, you'll always win if you wait in faith. This, my friend, is the game called *Life*.

A Prayer From Dacia

I was caught between hope and despair during my *valley* season and searched for material that would help me through this stage of life. I read a plethora of books with powerful testimonies that truly encouraged me; however, I discovered that most of them concluded with triumphant victories. Although I love a happy ending, what I find most uplifting is the witness of those who are presently still weathering the storm.

Since it appeared that there were few books that spoke directly to those that were still trekking the *valley* roads, I decided to write one. This book is for those of us who are currently smack dab in the middle of our waiting season. I hope you close this book with the reassurance that you are not the only person feeling the burden of delayed promises. I am still contending, still believing, and still trusting God just like some of you.

No matter how much I love God, I am not exempt from the trials of life. Therefore, I always have to remind myself that God never said weapons wouldn't form against me; He said that they would not prosper (Isaiah 54:17). So, in challenging times, I make a point to thrust myself into God's word and release it all to Him. I have to because *this* is what sustains me. *This* is what gets me through those seasons of waiting.

That being said, if you're in a season where you find it difficult to hold on, I've got you covered with a few devotionals in the back of this book. On days when life seems hard and waiting gets tough—grab this book, flip to the end, and let's choose to release every weight that accompanies our wait. Let's trust that God can carry the load better than we can. I leave you with these words from a poem (now a hymn) written by Joseph M. Scriven:

Oh, what peace we often forfeit

Oh, what needless pain we bear

All because we do not carry

Everything to God in prayer

Let's pray . . .

Lord, I pray for every person whose hands touch this book. I pray that Your supernatural anointing and blessing fall upon us like the morning dew. You said in Isaiah 26:3 that *You will keep in perfect peace, all whose mind is stayed on You because they confidently trust in You.*

We firmly stand on that word, choosing to trust you, knowing that *those who believe you without seeing will be blessed* (John 20:29 NLT). Therefore Lord, help us to trust You when we don't feel You near.

And for those of us that are wavering in faith, I ask that You increase our faith during this waiting season. We cry out Lord we *believe please help our unbelief,* our constant doubts, and our insecurities (Mark 9:20).

Illuminate our eyes Dad so that we can witness You working behind the scenes in our lives. When our faith is rattled by the storm and seeds of agnosticism creep in, I pray that you will always send an earthly messenger to confirm Your Word in our spirit and remind us that we haven't missed a beat and we are on the right path. When fears torment us, Father, raise up a standard against them for You *have not given us a spirit of fear but of power, love, and a sound mind* (2 Timothy 1:7).

I cancel the assignments of the enemy against our minds and I bind up the spirit of depression, oppression, jealousy, comparison, fear, and abandonment. We release the weight of this season and cast our cares on You. Lord, You have NOT forgotten us, and our best is yet to come. Tear down the barriers and walls that we have erected due to disappointment. Reveal the areas of fear that are causing us to trust You less. We know that *all things are working together for our good* because Your Word says it in Romans 8:28. We choose to believe that all things are possible through You (Matthew 19:26). And You will not disappoint as Your Word says in Romans 10:11. Do whatever it takes to build our faith. And when moments of despair come to try us, help us to recall Your goodness and graciousness towards us for You are indeed a *Good, Good Father.*

I close this prayer in the name of my Lord and Savior, Christ Jesus, AMEN!

The Rules of Engagement

We live in a society where it is the social norm to ask questions when engaging in casual conversation; especially upon meeting someone for the first time. Questions like: What do you do for a living? Are you married? What does your spouse do? Do you have kids? These are just to name a few. No harm, no foul, right? Wrong!

The truth is the climate has changed. The culture shifted and what was conventional 60 years ago is no longer viewed as status quo. People are moving out of their parent's house later in life, getting married later in life, and ultimately having children later in life. So, what used to be considered common sense "next steps" is now a bit more complicated due to obstacles along the journey. Yet, that still doesn't stop individuals from asking questions that pertain to one's personal life.

Our bout with conception is something we would have never written in our life plan, but this process has taught me to be ever so careful with my words. Let's be honest, some folks fly off at the mouth foolishly with no consideration or second thought of the words that left their tongue. While others stay on a "need-to-know" basis, living as private people and choosing not to ask questions they wouldn't want to be asked. I have become the latter, curbing my tongue for fear of offending someone with callous, casual talk. Why? Because I have borne the brunt of numerous invasive questions and assumptions pertaining to fertility that left me flabbergasted at the audacity of people. And I know I am not alone.

To those that are heedless of the offense: I forgive you, not because you need to know that you offended me, but because I needed to say it for myself. And please forgive me for any estranged relationships or missed baby showers due to distancing myself for my own sanity. This is one of the most vulnerable places a person can be so if you stumble upon yourself in this book, find no malice in my story. Instead, receive it as insight on what a person struggling with infertility or any other waiting season may be experiencing.

That being said, I feel it is my duty to issue what I'd like to call *The Rules Of Engagement*. Let me share some practical ways to ensure *Etiquette 101* is applied to your conversation with couples whose personal lives are foreign to you. Even though these rules stem from our personal experience with people asking about kids, feel free to apply these gems as a general rule of thumb. Now, let's enjoy some chuckles here and there as we dive into some intentional and some unintentional impudent behavior. I can't make this stuff up!

Rule #1

Get A Clue

While I was attending a friend's baby shower, I happened to sit by two Chatty Pattys who felt the need to ask everyone at our table *21 questions*. I tried to avoid eye contact at all cost, but I knew my turn was coming. I had already drafted my answers in advance to shut down the baby inquiries. (For the sake of following the storyline, we will name them Chatty and Patty.)

Patty: Oh my gosh, I love your ring!

Me: Thank you! (Yup, here it comes. That was the warm-up question.)

Chatty: How long have you been married?

Me: Seven years.

Patty: Oh Wow! Congrats!

Chatty: You have kids?

Me: Nope. Not yet. (Turns head to avoid further interrogation)

Chatty: Well, what are you waiting for?

Me: (Looks at Chatty with a plastic smile and answers) JESUS!

Patty: (Smiles, nods, and turns to engage with her neighbor)

Chatty: Huh? JESUS? Umm…okay! (Shrugs her shoulders)

It is clear that Patty got the hint and deflected to the nearest stranger to avoid further scavenging. Her polite smile of sympathy and nod affirmed that she understood. Chatty, on the other hand, was dumbfounded and disregarded my answer in dissatisfaction. I guess she didn't believe in Jesus. HA!

But wait, there's more! Moments after Chatty silently shunned my response, the host asked that each of us stand and bless the mom-to-be with kind words. A young lady stood up with tears drawing near and confessed that she and the mom-to-be had conceived around the same time and shared in excitement during their first trimester. Unfortunately, she had a miscarriage. She shared these words to the mom-to-be:

"You were so gracious. I know it had to have been awkward for you to share your special moments with me for fear of being insensitive but thank you for being a great friend. I'm excited for you. My mom and I (points to mom) absolutely adore you."

Skrrr! WAIT ONE MINUTE. Did she just point to…? YUP! The young lady's mom was none other than Chatty! Of all the people, how did Chatty not get a clue? After such devastation with her own daughter, it baffled me that she didn't pick up on the indicators to cease fire on questions. Is it just me that gets this rule? NO!

A friend of mine shared this story and it is so befitting to further drive the point. I told you these *Rules of Engagement* are universal. Here's a classic example of when someone didn't *Get*

A Clue and things went sour.

"My sister decided to bring her male-friend home this Christmas to meet the family. Like most families, we engaged in small talk to get to know the young fellow. I noticed (as well as most of the room) that he mentioned his older brother a few times; many of which were depicted in the past tense like "he was" or "he used to." The majority of the room steered clear of further babble about his brother (for fear of the inevitable), but my mother did not pick up on the clues and proceeded to ask: "Well, how is your brother now?" The room went silent. The male friend said, "Oh, he is deceased." You could hear a pin drop. We all sat in awkwardness as I watched the air leave my mother's lungs. Talk about embarrassment. All because she DIDN'T GET A CLUE!"

Observation is key. It's important to pick up on context clues when carrying on conversations with people; especially if a person is reluctant to divulge the detail or is pivoting on a subject matter. Chances are you've triggered an uncomfortable topic.

What do you do? Stop asking questions Inspector Gadget! Body language tends to tell a bigger story than our mouths can ever express. If you are an inquisitive conversationalist, follow the other person's lead to avoid heedless chatter. They will invite you into their business if they want you to know. All you have to do is simply watch and listen.

Get A Clue!

Rule #2

No Need To ASSume

We all know the saying, "Assuming makes you look like the first three letters of the word." Therefore, if we are aware of the validity of this statement, then why are we walking around partaking in bona fide donkeyism.

As a big jolt of "get your butt into gear, Dacia, and finish this book," I decided to release an online snippet of my mini-documentary on our struggles with infertility, entitled EXPOSED. This was huge for me because it was my first time admitting to the masses that we were struggling to conceive. I didn't go into great detail in the video clip so I had a feeling it would prompt friends and loved ones to chime in with their advice. Needless to say, this happened...

(Sarah's text message)
Hey, my love! Sorry to text you so late. Hope y'all are doing great!!! I struggled with infertility with my last two. I met a Chinese lady and she told me to take these prenatal vitamins (sends picture). I was pregnant before I finished the bottle. Coincidentally I shared these vitamins with three other ladies and they all got pregnant too. Give them a try. ♡ 🙏

(To which I replied)
Hey sis. Thanks so much boo. I appreciate it but ACTUALLY it isn't me.

(Sarah)

😐 Well, tell your friend

(Me)

Yeah, most people assume that the fertility issues lie with the woman but in fact, 35% of males deal with infertility. Do the math.

(Sarah)

OHHHHH! I just got my foot in my whole mouth!

(Me)
Yup! You and everybody else.

This, my friend, is a prime example of what not to do. To this day, I wonder how that toe-jam sandwich tasted. She assumed I was the one in the marriage facing infertility issues when in fact, I wasn't. It's insensitive to relate the malfunction to the female or better yet, to even assume anyone is at fault when one-third of infertility cases are unexplained. As you can see, assumptions are dangerous regardless of the scenario. Don't believe everything you *think*. I will sum up this rule with a quote from the incomparable Bishop T.D. Jakes, "Ignorance is brought about by assumptions."

No Need To ASSume.

Rule #3

Limit Offering Unsolicited Advice

What works for one does not always work for another. Offering unsolicited advice gives the notion that someone knows more about my situation than I do. I'm not sure what part of "not yet" or "we are working on it" is a license for people to offer advice to help us "nail it." Most of the time I want to ask my unsolicited advice-givers, "Remind me again where you got your degree in infertility from?" Here is the golden rule: If we don't ask, don't offer. Clear as mud.

I can write an entire book on this topic alone. Instead of filling this chapter up with a slew of stories on this, let's have a Self-Reflection Break. Have you broken Rule #3 by saying one of the following?

1. You're young. You have plenty of time.

2. You're running out of time. Your clock is ticking.

3. The Lord might be calling you to adopt. Have you considered adoption?

4. Do it every night, even when *Aunt Flo* arrives. Just grab a towel.

5. It will happen. Just relax. Get a glass of wine, take a bubble bath, and don't stress about it. As soon as you stop trying, it will happen.

6. You probably waited too long. Look into IVF.

7. Gravity can work against you. It's all about the sexual positions. Missionary and doggie-style are your best options to increase your chances.

8. After sex, lay on your back with your legs elevated. It increases your odds. It worked for me.

9. Change to a vegan diet or, on the other extreme, eat grass-fed beef.

10. Take Mucinex during ovulation.

11. Spin around, touch your toes, and clap three times.

And the list of *nonsense* keeps going.

Are you guilty of saying any of the above? Be honest, it's okay! What you have to recognize is that your line of questioning or suggestions, even if your questioning stems from concern, can be offensive.

Although it might be in your nature to want to help, please understand that infertility is a tough topic in and of itself. Not to mention, I don't want to know the positions you think we should be in to enhance our chances of conception and I surely don't want a visual of you in that position! Some things are just OFF

LIMITS. Keep it to yourself.

In my opinion, this goes for all walks of life. I'm sure all my single ladies (and gentlemen) can attest to this rule too. How many of you are forced to listen to people's how-to manual on finding a mate after finding out that you are single?

1. Here's the time where you need to focus on you.

2. Girl put on that red dress and high heels and come out from behind those four walls and you'll find him.

3. Get on a dating app. Have you tried _____? It worked for my friend _____. They are happily married now. Get on there.

Then, once you start dating, everyone becomes an expert presenting tips and tricks on how to keep the relationship vibrant. Why do people give unwarranted advice anyway? All the person said was that they're single. How does that somehow send a green light signal to the "advice-givers" that it's primetime to barrage the single person with unsolicited advice? Some of us are guilty of it and we have to do better.

I'm not saying don't offer advice; I'm suggesting waiting to be asked before pouncing at the chance to submit expertise on a given matter.

Those going through a waiting season could be made to feel as if they are not taking the proper steps to live out their situation; even though they are the ones going through it.

Therefore, while it usually comes from a good place, hold on to your counsel; just hold it. We just might ask you for it, but if we don't …

Limit Offering Unsolicited Advice.

Rule #4

Loose Lips Sink friendShips

A burden shared is a burden halved; therefore, it is an honor to be deemed trustworthy with one's secrets. A person with a proven track record of being a good listener and reliable safe haven is a prominent candidate to lighten your load. But the key component that separates good listeners and great friends is discretion. That's right. A tight-lipped friend makes for a blanket of open conversation.

"Lewis, party of eight. Lewis, party of eight." The waitress finally called our table. Friends were in town and my husband vowed to meet up with them downtown for dinner and conversation. Most of them were his close friends from years past and I have grown to love them like play cousins as well. When I first met Layla, we instantly clicked. She was hilarious. We were two peas in a pod! Of course, I sat across from her at the dinner table because I knew she would be the one I conversed with the most. Our catch up was long overdue.

The table topics swung from politics to sports and now we were on vacation spots. One of the fellas suggested that we head to the mountains soon for some skiing. Everyone at the table agreed that it would be fun. While in agreement, Layla's husband, Evan, burst out, "But ain't y'all trying to have a baby?" Forks fell, drinks settled and if looks could kill, someone would have dropped dead. I thought to myself, Who the *%&

(bleep) told him? Then I remembered. A few months prior, I told Layla about our fertility struggles over lunch. I needed to vent, and she was a great listener so, at the time, she seemed like a safe ear to land.

By the look on my face, it was now evident to her that she made a whoopsie. That was not to be shared. Layla turned to Evan and gave him a glare. I think she kicked him under the table because he had the "what did I do?" face.

Shortly after his blabber, the comments from the other patrons started:

"You guys are trying to have a baby?"

"Since when?"

"You remember John? He and his wife are trying too."

I let my husband respond as I sat in silence, furious that my confidante was a snitch. I *ASSumed* the information that I revealed to her was confidential, but clearly there was a pillow talk clause when it came to her significant other. It wasn't that Evan was privy to the information; it was that he didn't have enough sense to not blurt it out at the table.

Here is where I express the importance of Rule #4. If you don't want to lose valuable people, think twice before recounting privileged information. A lot of friendships have been unsalvageable due to a lack of discretion and I'm sorry, there is no spousal immunity rule. Telling a spouse is still considered a violation of privacy. Don't spill your friends' beans to anyone without getting approval. It's as painless as asking "do you care if I share this with _____." Unfortunately, Layla isn't the only culprit. Needless to say, I share very little with those who have difficulty keeping mum.

Secrets are bonds that bring people together. Trust is paramount when building relationships, so to be on the safe side, consider all intel confidential until otherwise noted. Respect others' privacy.

Remember, **Loose Lips Sink friendShips.**

Rule #5

Refrain From Asking People Their
AGE

How old are you (if you don't mind me asking)? It's the loaded question that seems to always follow my answer to not having kids yet. Yes, I do mind you asking. If I do tell you my age, will you then try to project your thoughts on the ticking of my biological clock? More times than not, yes, that's what happens. And for what? How does it help? If anything, it subjects me to the stressors of a performance metric. Not to mention, who really wants to discuss malfunctioning sex organs with a stranger or even a family member?

Chances are your motives are pure when asking someone's age, but not all inquisitors give the impression of being innocent. Shaming is a prominent reason why people are reluctant to admit their age. If a person chooses not to disclose their age, it is not always because they are ashamed of their age. It very well might be that they are afraid of being shamed or judged for their age and stage of life. Who wishes to be the focus of ageism?

A family member had recently graduated and we flew into town for the celebration. The house was full of people and the kitchen counter was flooded with enough food to feed a football team. I was inside chatting when a friend of the honoree walked in the door. She was tall and slender carrying the most adorable little girl on her hip. I surmised it was her daughter, but it turns out it was her niece. I estimated the little girl to be two or three years old, of clear walking age, but she clung to her aunt's hip like a clip on a potato chip bag. It was clear the weight of the little girl was overbearing as the woman moved across the room with a mean limp adjusting the little girl's weight as needed. Legs wrapped tight around her aunt, she refused to be put down and refrained from fraternizing with any unwanted greeters. I knew exactly how she felt though; she was among strange people. I, knowing some of these people, wouldn't have minded a hip to cling to myself and I'm grown.

The time had finally come for the woman to make a plate of food. I was curious as to how she would maneuver around the spread with the load on her hip. She tried, but finally, she bent over and stood the little girl up on the floor. She was on the verge of a wail when her aunt looked at her and said, "Wait a minute, okay, I'm going to fix us some food real quick." With a somber face, the little girl scowled over the room of thirty plus people. She locked eyes with me and proceeded to walk across the kitchen into the living room to yours truly with her arms extended. I was stumped. I had never met this child in my life but I guess she had an inclination of who was sane in the room. Of course, this became the topic of conversation as if a bouquet was tossed and it was my time to pop out a baby. "Oh wow,

Dacia," muttered one aunt. "Did she just come straight to you?" chimed a cousin. I replied, "I guess so." It's no secret, everyone knows I'm great with kids. Even kids sense it.

I picked up the little girl and put her on my hip, bouncing her in a playful manner, as she giggled to relay she had made the right decision. From across the room, I heard the chatter of the two relatives. One pried, "Umm, Dacia! How old is your husband?" As if she didn't know; she was his younger cousin. I knew that wasn't the real inquiry. She was using his age to calculate mine. I'm not stupid. I was hesitant to respond but I obliged to tickle her nosey fancy. And boy, was I right because I heard the aunt whisper to the cousin under her breath, "Well, what is she waiting on?"

This was their subtle (not so subtle) way of querying my age, and unfortunately in judgment and shame for my lack of having kids. Every part of me wanted to let the gates of hell prevail and light them up, but I pretended I didn't hear a word and continued my charades with my newfound toddler buddy. I knew their assumption was that I was closing in on the ideal age for childbearing. The nerve of them! My age was not their business and neither was my uterus. Mind Your Own Uterus!

Not every request for age is as atrocious as the one above, but predicaments like this draw hesitancy from people when asked that question. Interestingly enough, during our adolescent years, this question was harmless. In fact, most of us were eager for the half-birthday so that we could blare that we were not just six but six and a half or eleven and a half. But nowadays, *ageism* exists, and we have subconsciously subscribed to societal stereotypes that incite negative judgments.

People say phrases like: *You're past your prime. What are you waiting on? Wow, you don't look fifty! You look great for your age!* They all carry undertones of ageism and effects can be damaging. The goal is to maintain good manners, be considerate of other people's feelings, and respect their privacy. For that reason, when mingling with seasoned saints or adults of varied ages, be mindful that what may be deemed an innocent question might pinch a nerve. Whether you have a reason for asking or you're just plain nosy, the answer doesn't tell you anything about the person, so—

Refrain From Asking People Their Age.

Rule #6

No Need To Relate. Limit Testimony Tuesdays

I believe there is a compassionate instinct built inside of every…well, most human beings. With that instinct comes an innate desire to connect, to relate, and to help others, especially those that are facing tumultuous times. In most cases, there isn't anything wrong with this approach, but there are some instances when an attempt to relate or encourage someone can go completely south causing more harm than good.

My good friend Morgan whom I mentioned at the beginning of the book was now on her second child. She was in town and while we were catching up, she felt the need to try to relate to my TTC journey.

Morgan: What's the update?

Me: We are still trying, girl.

Morgan: I know the feeling; it took us a while to get pregnant the second time.

Me: Oh yeah, how long?

Morgan: 3 months!

Me: Mmm.

I thought to myself, "Really, girl? There are couples out there that have been trying to conceive for three, four, five … ten years. Get out of here!" Of course, I don't think she realized how insensitive the comment was, so I kindly moved on to the next topic. Not to dismiss her personal journey at all; but, three months compared to six years? Yeah, sorry, I can't relate. I walked away more annoyed than inspired.

Then there's the surplus of Testimony Tuesdays. Shortly after voicing to a family member that we were facing fertility issues she immediately recalled a "testimony" from a fellow church member.

"You know Sherrie, right?" she said.

"Hmm," I thought for a second, but quickly recognized I had no idea who Sherrie was.

She continued, "Well, Sherrie and her husband were trying to conceive for several years to no avail. Sherrie's sister Jenn fell on hard times resulting in her kids being taken away from her. Thankfully, Sherrie and her husband took in her sister's three kids and wouldn't you know it, as soon as she adopted those kids Sherrie got pregnant! Look at God!"

Wait, WHAT? This was not inspiring to me AT ALL. Indeed, this is a great testimony and praise God for it, but how is this invigorating to me? What is the common denominator as it pertains to my journey? Was she telling me I needed to take in three kids and then I would miraculously conceive biological children? I was so confused and again, annoyed.

Lord knows everyone has a story to tell—some of which should remain untold. For the record, I really do love to hear stories of triumph; who doesn't? However, be careful in expressing how a family member, friend, or co-worker conceived as a way to give *us* hope.

Some of these so-called "success stories" people share are horror stories. They're not always about conception either. Take this one for instance:

My friend Nicole just turned thirty-five and made up her mind at an earlier age that she was going to wait until she was married to have sex. While we attended a dinner, another friend Jasmine decided it was Testimony Tuesday and offered up words of encouragement when the topic of marriage and children came up. "I know this woman who kept her virginity until she was married. She waited forever, but finally got married at forty-six and is having her first child." Nicole looked at Jasmine and said, "That is not my portion!" I gagged on my water and shook my head.

Again, how was this testimony helpful? Did she imply that this would happen for Nicole too in about ... ooh eleven years? How is this fitting? From the lack-luster look on Nicole's face, she was not optimistic or enthused by what was implied.

It's subconscious because it's a part of human nature to want to make a person feel better. There is nothing wrong with sharing testimonies; success stories are sensational. They can offer a sense of hope to a dismal situation. Just make sure that it relates and that the person is receptive to it. Gauge their demeanor and proceed with caution.

My personal suggestion is to offer a different way to console a friend facing hard times. Sometimes silence is better than trying to relate or share information that can possibly make them feel worse.

There is…**No Need To Relate. Limit Your Testimony Tuesdays**.

Rule #7

Everything Can't Be Divine Punishment

What goes around comes around. What you put out in the universe will come back to you. Karma is a—bleep. Karma never loses an address. You create your own fate by your actions. You reap what you sow. We've heard them all, and in most cases believe them to be accurate. We've also seen great people become the beneficiary of unfortunate situations that leave us wondering, "Why do bad things happen to good people?"

In the quest to make sense of tragedy or heartbreak, it is natural to try to find reasons for the misfortune that happened. Therefore, we twist or distort the perception of God by determining that a person has done something wrong to invoke a subsequent deserved penalty from God. It's the law of cause and effect at play in people's heads. This type of reasoning soothes the psyche from the aches of the unknown and leads people to find blame in the unexplained; even if it's furthest from the truth.

For instance, when I mentioned our fertility struggles to a devout Christian, the first question that proceeded out of their mouth was, "Did you have an abortion?" This question was indicative that all infertility is a consequence of aborting a child. I have never had an abortion and couldn't believe this was their initial thought. The nerve!

I was led to believe that it was their religion and views on abortion that brought them to this conclusion. But to suggest that abortion would constitute infertility is preposterous. In fact, I know several women who made the choice to have an abortion(s) in their younger years who now have beautiful, healthy children. Let's be clear, there is no medical research that definitively links abortions to infertility. I hate to burst their bubble, but not all adverse situations are repercussions of a presumed preceding action that is deemed wrong (sinful) in the eyes of others.

Take for example, when Kobe Bryant died unexpectedly in a plane crash, the world was in a state of shock. The masses were mystified on how something like this could happen to a beloved husband and father. The media debacle came when some people thought this calamity was a punishment from God for his alleged assault charge in 2003; thus, insinuating that divine retribution was the catalyst to the loss of his life. How would that explain why God killed eight others to be punished along with him? It just doesn't make sense.

God is not going around sounding the trumpet of doom and penalizing people with affliction. A Loving Father doesn't do that. God does not wish that anyone should *perish* (2 Peter

3:9). God gives good gifts (James 1:7). He is light and in Him, there is no darkness at all so He cannot be good and evil (1 John 1:5). Yes, God allows things because He is Sovereign but let us never forget that we have an adversary whose sole mission is to kill, steal, and destroy (John 10:10). There is no need for divine punishment in tragic ways when God has the ability to cut us off and stop us from breathing right now.

I'll wrap it up with this: There is a correspondence with the choices we make and the consequences that follow, but there is not a direct connection to transgression and tribulation. We will never be able to comprehend why misfortune comes upon some harder than others. Therefore, let us not be quick to erroneously *ASSume* that someone's plight is a direct correlation to wrongdoing (in your eyes) …

Everything Is Not Divine Punishment.

Rule #8

T.H.I.N.K. Before You Speak

Have you experienced conversations where someone asked the unfathomable like: *What are you (regarding race/ethnicity)? Whatever happened to (insert ex's name)? Have you gained (or lost) weight? When are you settling down? When are you starting a family? Is that your real hair?* None of which are socially graceful, so throwing an apology before an offense like, "forgive me" or "pardon me for asking," doesn't make the insult hurt any less.

The words that come out of our mouths expose one of two things: our level of intelligence or our level of ignorance. Sometimes it's best to say nothing at all, but if we are going to speak it is imperative that we pay regard to the emotional potency of our words, as they can cause colossal damage to one's well-being. If you think it might be insensitive, that's a telltale sign that it probably is insensitive. I believe if we stop navigating conversations through the lenses of our own experiences, we will avoid unintentionally judging and shaming people whose walk is foreign to us.

Let me be clear, I am not saying we have to tread lightly in all of our conversations; I'm saying tread lightly knowing words have an impact. Fight the urge to ask probing questions and embrace thoughtfulness first. Follow their lead; they will invite you into the areas of their life that they're comfortable confessing. Active listening will guide you and keep you out of the line of fire.

To sum it up, the overarching rule for this entire section is T.H.I.N.K. before you speak. It's as simple as *stop, drop, and roll.* To ensure we are being Conscious Conversationalist before we utter a word, let's ask ourselves:

T–is it TRUE?

H–is it HELPFUL?

I–is it INSPIRING?

N–is it NECESSARY?

K–is it KIND?

Remember the words you speak can only be forgiven not forgotten. Therefore, if you only take one thing from this chapter of the book, let it be this: "Be quick to listen and slow to speak" (James 1:19). It just might save someone an extra trip to the therapist.

Think Before You Speak!

THE GAME OF LIFE

14-Day Devotional

Day One

The Waiting Game

In recent months, Tik Tok Challenges have become a fad. What was once ostracized as an app for kids who had too much time on their hands has now crossed over into all demographics, thanks to the global pandemic known as Covid–19. One of the most adorable challenges that went viral on Tik Tok was the Fruit Snack Challenge, also known as the Patience Challenge or Candy Challenge. Basically, this game encourages parents to test their child's self-restraint.

It's simple; parents put a bowl of snacks or delicious treats in front of their kid and tell them they can eat it once they get back to the room. The parent leaves and the game begins. What makes this most amusing is the undetected camera recording the kid's every move. I must say this made for fantastic TV. Some children epically failed and forfeited the rest of their snack while others passed their patience test with ease enjoying their savory reward in exchange.

My absolute favorite of this challenge was of a baby girl named Niko. While undergoing the delayed gratification challenge, there was a moment when her countenance fell as if her time to indulge in her favorite snack would never come. The best part came at the end of the video when she randomly looked over her shoulder and a spark of enthusiasm prompted her to start jumping in her seat. We, the viewers, didn't know why her patient stance turned into pure joy, but we later learned that Niko heard her father before she saw him and knew it was time to feast on the promise.

Watching this video of Niko reminded me of another girl's experience with the waiting game:

I had been anticipating it for weeks, counting down the days until the weekend, and Friday was finally here. Whenever I spent the weekend with him, I had the time of my life; food, fun, and lots of surprises. There I stood at the front porch, veins full of excitement, and bags packed at the door.

I figured I'd hang outside since I knew it would be a short wait but the hands on the clock told a different story.

"Mom," I yelled inside. "What time is he coming?"

"I don't know sweetheart. He didn't say," she replied. This was unusual, unheard of, out of the ordinary. He was never late. I rushed inside to call. No answer. I felt my heart breaking as nightfall approached. Did he forget about me?

My tearstained face met my hands, catching each droplet in my palm when suddenly the sound of laughter interrupted my cry. I gazed across the street just in time to see my childhood friend jump into the arms of her father. He swung her around in circles as she reveled at his arrival. A blow of envy silenced my tears. Why couldn't that be me?

Any lingering hope began to taper away with the sun, and as it set on the horizon, abandonment settled in my soul. My heart sank deeper at the notion that the unthinkable had happened. Yup, forgotten by the one I loved the most.

I pulled the screen door behind and resolved to close the big door when the faint sound of an engine crescendoed in my ear. I looked over my shoulder and saw a car in the deep distance. My heart raced as my emotions u-turned into anticipation and excitement as it got closer and closer. It was him. He finally showed.

Suddenly, my biggest fear was annihilated by the evidence in front of my very own eyes. He headed towards me with a big smile on his face and a teddy bear in his hand. I hugged his neck as if my life depended on it saying, "You remembered!"

"Of course I did," he replied. "I told you I was coming. I just didn't tell you the time I was coming."

It was clear from the stories above that patience is indeed a virtue, but what was most satisfying was each girl's reaction when they realized their fathers didn't forget about them. Yes, the wait seemed long, especially for a young child—five minutes feels like five months to them. Nevertheless, when it was all said and done and they heard their fathers approaching, their expectations grew. It was worth the wait.

Winning the waiting game of life takes patience as well. But while you are waiting, know, without a shadow of a doubt, that your heavenly Father has not abandoned you. You are not forgotten. Just listen for the sound of your Father and soon you will look over your shoulder and shout with glee in anticipation. Not to mention, you might even get to relish in some yummy fruit snacks for passing the test.

In your wait . . . release the weight of impatience. God has not forgotten you. Trust His timing and wait with expectation.

Let's Weigh In

Are there any areas of your life where you are failing the patience challenge? If so, list them in the margin.

What is God asking you to do in those areas after reading this devotional?

<u>Scriptures</u>

I would have despaired had I not believed that I would see the goodness of the Lord in the land of the living. Wait for and confidently expect the Lord; Be strong and let your heart take courage; Yes, wait for and confidently expect the Lord (Psalm 27:13-14 AMP).

Rest in the Lord, and wait patiently for Him, Those that wait upon the Lord, they shall inherit the land (Psalms 37:7, 9).

<u>Prayer</u>

Abba Father, forgive me for the times I have been impatient for You are not slow in keeping your promises. Help me not to jump ahead of Your plans out of frustration. Increase my ability to tolerate the wait with the understanding that You are orchestrating the perfect plan for my life. I am not forgotten. I am not forsaken. I will patiently wait (in expectation) for Your goodness. In Jesus' Name.

Day Two

Angry Birds

Have you ever played Angry Birds? In case you haven't, Angry Birds is a Smartphone game that broke all kinds of video game records back in 2010. The premise boils down to this: the birds are furious because the pigs stole their eggs. On a mission to seek vengeance, they run the risk of ruining their own lives by slingshotting themselves into the exterior of the pigs' fort in an effort to dismantle their dwelling. A tad bit extreme, but anger can incite a myriad of outrageous outbursts.

Anger is a complex, yet natural human emotion that shows itself in various ranges and behaviors. This can range from a retaliating leader firing off revenge tweets in place of missiles, to the pouting of a toddler not getting candy.

When I got really mad as a kid, I would throw temper tantrums that usually landed me in even more trouble. These irate eruptions quite often emerged when things didn't turn out the way I hoped. Although people can be the catalyst that sparks this emotion within, life's misfortunes can be another impetus that flips this switch. Truthfully, I still have a few of those outbursts as an adult. Every now and again—when I'm home alone, of course—you can find me yelling, screaming, crying, and slinging paper across the room (since it doesn't break) to relieve the stings of a *hurting heart.*

That's right, I believe anger derives from hurt and sadness. Anger is simply a great sense of displeasure or annoyance. It's frustration. I'm going to refer back to *Angry Birds* again (the movie this time) for the sake of this lesson since the writers did a great job honing in on some root causes of anger with their central character, Red.

Red was a bit of an outcast, perceived to be the only grumpy bird on Bird Island—*the cheeriest place in the world.* However, Red had good reason to be upset. The poor guy never caught a break. Red was disparaged for not having parents and constantly ridiculed for his remarkably thick eyebrows, leaving him lonely and friendless. Needless to say, his pessimistic attitude spawned at the hand of pain, sorrow, and rejection. When Red tried to turn over a new leaf in hope for better, fate inevitably would kick back and greet him with a stroke of bad luck. Eventually, Red's unaddressed emotions, and unfavorable occurrences resorted to deep embitterment, isolation, and a cynical outlook on life.

Can you relate? I know I can.

There have been several times when life sucker-punched me with unexpected delays and heartbreaking ordeals that left me in a stupor of grief and anger. And just when I mustered up enough hope to believe for a different outcome, I would be coldcocked with another set of luckless nuances. Hence, I would allow my agitation with life to escort me into a state of anger and isolation; and like Red, I wanted nothing more than to be left alone. This behavior is a typical reflex for people with seemingly undeserved encounters in life.

Let's pivot here and take a look at the character Job in the Bible. Job was a faithful servant of God who was hit with a succession of unfavorable circumstances that would leave most barely hanging on to sanity. First, he was robbed of his life savings, then his servants were struck by lightning; and if that wasn't enough all ten of his children died in a natural disaster. Don't miss the most comprehensive part of this story; all of these calamities happened within a span of a few minutes. Yes, I said *minutes* (Job 1:13-19)!

Unfortunately, his troubles didn't end there. Shortly after burying his kids, a poor and grieving Job was afflicted with terrible boils that covered his entire body. I don't know many people that would have survived these horrid realities. If anyone had good reason to be angry at the injustices of life, hands down, it was Job. And angry, he was. He ranted and raved throughout the next thirty-eight chapters trying to make sense of a good God who allowed bad things to happen to him. What I love about this story the most is that God listened. He welcomed Job's honesty.

Many of us have been (or still are) angry and asking God questions similar to that of Job's. And guess what? God welcomes our impassioned rants as well. What I have learned over the years is that retreating to my corner and pouting never heals the hurt that begat the anger. The restorative process of anger actually befalls when I candidly express my distress to God and seldom those anger sessions are full-out hissy fits. I'm sure God has a field day watching my episodes. I imagine Him kicked back with some popcorn chuckling as I whine and complain about my term of injustices. But I know one thing for sure, God embraces every part of my pain and is eager to heal my hurt.

I'm here to tell you that there is nothing wrong with being angry, but unchecked anger has the potential to turn into bitterness, bitterness into resentment, and resentment into disdain. The truth is God did not promise a life immune from hurts, disappointments, and defeats; although, He did promise to always be there for us.

So, if and when life hands you a dose of suffering (death, disease, loss, or pain) that makes you unhappy and angry, remember the goal is to never let those disappointments get you to a point where you start wreaking havoc on your own life. If you are angry at God, tell Him. Keep the lines of communication wide open. Lay your heart before God. He honors your transparency, so trust Him with your anguish.

When we admit our aggravations, God will buff away that anger and like Red at the end of *Angry Birds* and Job in the Bible, you will overcome your past afflictions. You will also find the courage you need to be optimistic and live a victorious life.

In your wait . . . release the weight of anger. Bring all of your frustrations before God and let Him heal the broken areas of your heart.

Let's Weigh In

Recall a time when something unfavorable happened in your life and you became angry with God.

Did this situation drive you to talk to God or distance yourself from Him?

<u>Scriptures</u>

Peace has been stripped away, and I have forgotten what prosperity is. I cry out, "My splendor is gone! Everything I had hoped for from the Lord is lost!" The thought of my suffering and homelessness is bitter beyond words. I will never forget this awful time, as I grieve over my loss. Yet I still dare to hope when I remember this: The faithful love of the Lord never ends! His mercies never cease. Great is his faithfulness; his mercies begin afresh each morning. I say to myself, "The Lord is my inheritance; therefore, I will hope in him!" (Lamentations 3:17-24 NLT).

Yet what we suffer now is nothing compared to the glory he will reveal to us later (Romans 8:18 NLT).

<u>Prayer</u>

Gracious Father, today I bring every hurt, disappointment, pain, and loss before You. I know that trials are a part of life's journey so forgive me for pointing a finger at You out of frustration. When anger arises from the adversities of life, show me how to run to You and not away from You. And when despair overrides optimism, restore my hope in Your Sovereign hand. In Jesus' Name.

Day Three

Last Word

While exploring the vibes of Nashville, my husband stumbled upon a spot called Game Point—a quaint cafe that promotes unplugging (from devices) and engaging in board games with family and friends. This place is magical with every game you can imagine, from beloved classics to the unheard-of. Either way, you are guaranteed to have an enjoyable night of entertainment.

After playing a few old school standards, we ventured out to a few games we were unaccustomed to—one being *Last Word*. Some of you might know this game but it was foreign to me. Although unfamiliar with the rules, I was confident that this was my type of game since having the *last word* is in my DNA.

The object of the game is to be the first to get your pawn to the finish line. Sounds easy, right? Well, in order to do so, each round you must be the *last* person to shout out words connected to a subject and letter card to advance; and, you have to do so before the random interval timer buzzes. Technically, it's a race to be last. The last to speak, that is.

I can think of two other times that many desire to have the *last word*; one being arguments; two being *life*. When it comes to the progression of our lives, we want the privilege of having the final word on how things will play out. I know I do! God will be so gracious to give me a glimpse of His big plan for my life and if things don't work out the way I think they should or in what I deem a timely fashion, you can often find me curating a plan of my own. Is anybody with me on this one?

I am well aware that I don't have the head-knowledge to understand God's perfect timing; therefore, patience is a constant prayer point for me. I am always eager to take the wheel of any obstacle that I don't see moving to the beat of my drum. The end result usually vacillates somewhere between a major disappointment and a monumental disaster. But I have to be honest, sometimes God appears to be as *slow as molasses* with His promises and unfortunately, my default mechanism during an extended waiting season is *self-reliance.*

Let's visit our friend Saul in the Bible to illuminate the detriment of taking matters into our own hands. In 1 Samuel 13, we find Saul and his soldiers gripped with fear in Gilgal as they prepare for battle against the Philistine army.

I must make it clear; this would not be an effortless match because the Philistines were mighty in number and ruthless in combat.

But, Samuel, the prophet of that day, told Saul to wait for him at Gilgal for seven days (1 Samuel 10:8). Once he returned, Samuel would offer the appropriate sacrifice to the Lord and release instructions on how Saul should proceed.

Four days passed. Five days came and went. The sixth day rolled by and still no Samuel. Panic settled within Saul's spirit when he witnessed his troops steadily retreating in fear of their *doomsday*. One glimpse at the enemy horde and they were shaking in their boots—clearly, they wanted no parts of this escapade.

With terror-stricken soldiers on one side and a massive enemy poised for an attack on his other side, Saul was desperate for a move from God. He grew tired of waiting for Samuel, and on the morning of the seventh day, Saul took matters into his own hands. He went ahead of Samuel and decided to offer the traditional sacrifices on his own and usurp the role of the priest, which was against God's law (Deuteronomy 12:5-14).

Just as Saul completed the offering, guess who arrived—on the seventh day—as promised? Samuel. Appalled by the foolhardiness of Saul, Samuel queried why he would do such a thing. Saul replied, "You didn't arrive when you said you would … so I was compelled to offer the burnt offering myself before you came" (1 Samuel 13:11-12).

As frustration builds, how many of you resolve to work matters out on your own and find that your impetuous actions lead to more disarray? I will definitely raise my hand here. Guilty! Having the last word and moving ahead of God isn't worth it.

When you feel under pressure or sense that time is running out, you may find yourself assessing whether or not you should bust a move or wait on God. Well, let me help you out on this one … wait. I know—easier said than done—but impatience can drive you to disobedience. Remember delayed doesn't mean denied. God could very well be testing your patience and obedience, so sit tight and expect God to show up—on time.

For those who are not familiar with Saul's story, you might be asking, "Dacia, what happened to Saul?" Well, my friend, Saul suffered tremendous consequences as a result of his constant disobedience and self-reliance. His defiance forfeited God's original plan for his life, and he was forced to settle for a life less desirable—all because he decided to rely on his own intelligence instead of waiting on God. Now as far as the battle at Gilgal, thank God for grace. God still came through for Saul and the Israelites, which is encouraging. Why? Because scripture says, "We may throw the dice, but the Lord determines how they fall" (Proverbs 16:33 NLT). To put it concisely, no matter how we look at it, God always has the *Last Word*. He is in complete control and sovereign over all. We may as well roll with His punches and submit to His plan.

In your wait . . . release the weight of self-reliance. Trust in the Lord's sovereignty. His timing is the best timing. His plan is the best plan.

Let's Weigh In

Are there any areas of your life where you find yourself being self-reliant instead of God-reliant? If so, list them.

Looking at the areas you wrote, what steps can you take to keep from taking matters into your own hands?

Scriptures

Jesus has the last word on everything and everyone, from angels to armies. He's standing right alongside God, and what he says goes (1 Peter 3:22 MSG).

Trust in the Lord with all your heart, And lean not on your own understanding; in all your ways acknowledge Him, And He shall direct your paths (Proverbs 3:5).

Prayer

Lord God above all, You are the orchestrator of every detail of my life. When I grow impatient with Your timing, help me to trust Your plan. When pressures weigh heavily on me and I am tempted to move ahead of You, steady my hand and guide my feet. Save me from myself so that I may rest in Your sovereignty. In Jesus' Name.

Day Four

Where's Waldo?

Where's Waldo? is a popular children's puzzle book by Martin Handford that probably kept you up all night searching for Waldo amongst an ocean of characters. With an extensive visual art accompanied by extreme detail in design on one page, it seemed impossible to find Waldo amidst the chaos. In my case, sometimes I'd get lucky and find him immediately and other times it took a while.

His characteristics are distinct and remain the same with each level of the game—red and white striped shirt and hat with black glasses. You would think this would make for an easy feat but instead quite the contrary. Each page is decked with a busy scene and anywhere between three hundred and five hundred eye-catching characters. This can make it challenging to detect his whereabouts. Therefore, in the quest to find Waldo, it is very important to remain focused, refusing to be distracted by the surrounding elements that can draw your attention away from him and cause you to miss him altogether.

For many of us, our waiting season can resemble a page out of a *Where's Waldo?* book. What initially appears to be an easy undertaking turns into an agonizing strain as we search for God amidst the surrounding madness. We know He is present but like the disciple Peter in Matthew 14 of the Bible, our focus can become diverted by the high waves and fierce winds (distractions) causing us to doubt God's presence.

Sometimes when in difficult situations, we allow ourselves to be overcome with paralyzing fear which blinds us from seeing Jesus in the situation, even though His characteristics are on display right in front of our eyes. We can easily miss His love, grace, forgiveness, peace, faith, and protection; consequently, like Waldo, we must know the characteristics of God in order to recognize Him.

When Peter saw Jesus walking on water he asked Jesus to permit him to join Him (Matthew 14:28). Peter's request was granted, and he was able to walk on the sea as long as he stayed focused on Jesus. However, Peter allowed distractions to interfere, changing his focus to the wind and waves (the surrounding elements). Ultimately, his faith faltered and he began to sink.

During *waiting seasons*, it can seem easier to focus on the odds that are stacked against us rather than the characteristics and power of our God. When we focus on these distractions, we too can fall into despair and sink. We must remember our *wait* is not bigger than our God. Don't focus on the circumstances around (what you see happening or not happening) but remain fixed on the task at hand—finding God in the wait. Adjust all focus back to the characteristics of God.

Similar to walking a tightrope, I believe each step of faith becomes more and more difficult; but rest assured God is with you. Just like in the game *Where's Waldo?*, once you find Waldo in the image you must turn the page and prepare to look for him at the next stage. With each page, there are more distractions making it harder and harder to find Waldo, nevertheless, he is still on the page, right there in front of your face with the same characteristics (red and white striped shirt and hat with black glasses). The only way to find him is to look for those same distinct characteristics found in the previous stage.

God is the *same yesterday, today, and forever* (Hebrews 13:8). His nature and characteristics are consistent no matter what we face. Trust that He is there. He is on the page. He will never leave or forsake you. Change your focus and you will find Him, for God is with you in your wait.

In your wait ... release the weight of distractions. Focus on the Problem Solver, not the problem. Keep your eyes on God in the midst of your storms.

Let's Weigh In

What are some distractions that cause you to doubt God's presence in your life?

Name three characteristics of God. Take a moment and reflect on how God has shown those characteristics during times of struggle.

<u>Scriptures</u>

Have I not commanded you? Be strong and of good courage; do not be afraid, nor be dismayed, for the Lord your God *is* with you wherever you go (Joshua 1:9).

Therefore, holy brothers … keep your focus on Jesus (Hebrews 3:1 ISV).

<u>Prayer</u>

Oh Lord, remove any distractions that have the potential to lead me into unbelief. Help me to keep my eyes fixed on You no matter what is going on around me. You are all-powerful. You are faithful. You are good. You are loving. You are just. You are merciful. You are holy. When the wind and the waves of life hit, remind me of these characteristics so that I can see You in my wait. In Jesus' Name.

Day Five

Mother May I?

Remember the age-old game *Mother May I?* One child assumes the lead role of Mother (or father) and stands across the yard facing away from the other players who are assembled at the start line. Each player takes turns asking, "Mother May I _____?" and proceeds to make the suggested movement. For example, Alice might ask, "Mother, may I take five steps forward?" The leader may then respond, "Yes, you may" or "No you may not but you may _____ instead," inserting his/her own command. Such as "Alice, you may take a baby step/ballerina step/giant leap/one-legged hop forward or backward." Ideally, each player hopes to receive a favorable answer from the leader to move closer to the goal, but that's not always the case. What is always the case is that the person who doesn't ask doesn't receive a promising answer, or an answer at all, for that matter.

Back in my high school years, when I wanted to do something, I had to get permission from my mom. When I asked for something, it was never with the hope of her telling me no. Quite the contrary—I asked because I believed that she would grant my request; that is, until I started driving. You see, my cousin taught me how to drive at a very young age on the backroads of Mississippi when I used to visit every summer. By the time I hit sixteen, I thought my skills behind the wheel were superb. But when I got my driver's license and bravely asked my mom if I could drive unsupervised, she hit me with "no you may not."

Of course, that didn't stop me from asking the following weekend … and the weekend after that. I started noticing a pattern. Month after month, every request to take the car for a spin was met with an astounding *no*. My mother wasn't budging, and I quickly saw that I wasn't breaking ground on the matter. Eventually, I lost hope and stopped asking.

During our spiritual walk, faith is often mixed with unbelief when request after request is denied. We get accustomed to *not* having our prayers answered in the way that we hoped they would and before long, we find ourselves with a perpetual prayer life with little to no expectation of God answering our supplications. I referred to this earlier in the book as an *unbelieving believer.*

It's not that we don't have faith, but that there has been enough disappointment to make us unsure if God will intervene. Case in point—that relationship we dedicated years to that didn't result in the future spouse we prayed for or that sick relative we sincerely hoped God would heal, but the illness prevailed or possibly took their life. Among other things, let's not forget about those marriages we earnestly believed to be restored that dissolved right before our very eyes. Yup! It's those not-so-happy endings we all dread that have the potential to wane our expectation of God showing up.

In Acts 12, the author Luke gives us a vivid picture of *unbelieving believers* when he recounts the miraculous deliverance of Peter. At the beginning of this chapter, we discover that King Herod—on a mission to persecute Christians—has executed James, the brother of John, and has now arrested Peter. Herod's plan to assassinate Peter next was impeded by a Jewish holiday celebration, resulting in Peter's trial being postponed. "Peter was therefore kept in prison, but constant prayer was offered to God for him by the church" (v. 5). Another version says, "the church went into a season of intense intercession asking God to free (Peter)" (TPT).

As the night before the execution approached, it became evident that Peter's situation was bleak. Surrounded by sixteen guards, it was near impossible for him to escape this doom. But I'd be remiss to not mention that while the saints were *fervently* praying for his release, Peter was sound asleep. (*Say what now?*) You mean to tell me the night before he was scheduled to be the victim of a guillotine, the brother was sound asleep? (*Yes, sleeping like a baby!*)

I don't know about you, but that's the kind of *peace* I want to walk in. No doubt about it, if that was me, I would have been wide awake, shaking in my boots, and vehemently praying for a lifeline. I now comprehend Peter's words written in 1 Peter 5:7:

"Casting all of your cares upon (God), for He cares for you." Peter grasped how to lay his *burdens* down. May we all take a page from Peter's book when confronted with the worries of this world.

In our story with Peter, we learn that God indeed answered the pleas of the church. In a divine rescue mission, an angel of the Lord appeared and rescued Peter from prison (vs. 6-10). After realizing this miracle was not a dream, Peter headed to the house of John Mark's mother, where the saints were gathered for prayer (v. 12).

Now, this is where the story gets funny—tickles me every time. When Peter knocked on the door, a young servant girl by the name of Rhoda got up to see who it was. She immediately recognized Peter's voice and ecstatically ran to tell the others, forgetting to open the door, leaving poor Peter standing outside. But listen to what the saints had to say when Rhoda shared the good news: "'You're out of your mind,' they told her. When she kept insisting that it was so, they said, 'It must be his angel'." (v. 15 NIV).

Here they are at the prayer meeting, petitioning for intervention from God, travailing all night for Peter's release; yet when he shows up, they don't believe it, slamming the door in the brother's face. Moreover, when they finally affirmed it was the real Peter, they were shocked and amazed.

Why were they surprised? Because they were praying to God but had very little expectation of Him answering their prayer—*unbelieving believers.*

In their defense, I am sure they prayed for James and other apostles who in spite of their supplications still suffered and conclusively died as martyrs. Unbelief had crept in and their spiritual expectations were lowered. So, I believe—based on their experience of others who suffered—these saints counted Peter *as good as dead.* Their hope, if any, was scanty of him being snatched from the door of death, and doubtful if God would help.

Our experiences weigh heavily on our ability to believe God for things. Sometimes we are afraid to even ask because we have been met with constant denial or delay of our requests. I can attest to that personally. During my waiting season, skepticism seeped in when asking God for my deepest desires. The heartache of my previous encounters caused me to not believe God for the impossible. Although I prayed for it, when I didn't see it materialize (on my timetable), I no longer anticipated it coming to fruition—an *unbelieving believer.*

I love this story in Mark chapter 9 of a father who is desperately seeking healing for his son. After several failed attempts, immense pain, and disappointment, you can sense the anguish in this father's petition when He entreated Jesus to heal his son. When Jesus asked the father if he believed He could heal his son, he confessed, "Lord I believe; help my unbelief!" In this statement, the father humbly acknowledges that although he wants to completely trust God, life has presented a hopeless predicament that has caused his faith to falter.

Life's saga of unremitting disappointments may tempt you to bottom out in hopelessness, but when belief and unbelief collide, refuse to let the unbelief take you under. When in the presence of doubt, first, acknowledge it like the father did in Mark 9:24. Second, ask God to increase your faith. Remember, faith is a gift from God (Ephesians 2:8,9) and He will help you to trust His plan. Lastly, get your ASK up—*ask* God for the impossible! Pray gutsy prayers and raise your expectations.

I will leave you with this: when a man asks for a woman's hand in marriage, I don't believe he is asking with the hope of her saying no. God wants us to approach Him with the same attitude and assurance. Bring your requests to the Lord—your *Father May I's*—and when you bring them, believe without a doubt that the Father will answer, "Yes, you may." If the answer is, "No, you may not," then trust Him enough to know that He will redirect you with, "but do _____ instead."

In your wait … release the weight of unbelief. All things are possible for those who believe. Get your ASK up and wait in expectation.

Let's Weigh In

Have you ever prayed for something but didn't really expect God to answer? If so, was your unbelief a result of previous disappointing experiences?

What are three things you are believing God for in this season of your life?

Write them on a sheet of paper or index card. Beneath your requests, write the scriptures, and place these cards on your mirror or wall. Recite them every day and wait in expectation.

Scriptures

In the morning, LORD, you hear my voice; in the morning I lay my requests before you and wait expectantly (Psalm 5:3 NIV).

Now this is the confidence that we have in Him, that if we ask anything according to His will, He hears us. And if we know that He hears us, whatever we ask, we know that we have the petitions that we have asked of Him (1 John 5:14-15).

Therefore I say to you, whatever things you ask when you pray, believe that ye receive *them*, and you will have *them* (Mark 11:24).

Prayer

Lord, forgive me for praying and not expecting You to answer. Help me to pray with assurance that You will fulfill my supplications with manifestation or direction. When I am faced with hopelessness and my faith falters, drive away every ounce of unbelief, and rekindle my hope in You. In the presence of doubt, let my weak faith cling to Your mighty hand. Give me a fixed attitude of trust and confidence. *Lord I believe; help my unbelief.* In Jesus' Name.

Day Six

Tug Of War

I was very ambitious growing up. Most of the activities I participated in called for some level of competitive edge. While in grade school, I always looked forward to Field Day. *Field Day* was the end-of-year send-off that the physical education department hosted, signaling school would soon be out for the summer. It was on this day that everyone got to strut their stuff and show off their athletic skills (or lack thereof).

There was something for everyone at field day: bean bag toss, potato sack race, Frisbee throw, broad jump, and the fifty-yard dash. None of which required the help of another participant. It was every person for themselves. These were, of course, my favorite activities because I had complete control, only relying on three things; me, myself, and I. The only game that I could not dominate alone was Tug Of War. This game was never intended to be conquered single-handedly; hence the reason I HATED it!

Most people assume that tug of war is a sport that only requires power and endurance, but in actuality, it is a technical sport requiring mechanics and strategy in order to be effective. This is executed with the help of what is known as a driver. Though not actually in the game, the *driver* directs their team on the exact moments to "pull" and exact moments to "hang" in order to prevail in victory.

When the driver notices that the opposition is attempting to pull, they call a "hang." The command "hang," also synonymous with the command "rest," may insinuate an order to chill out, disengage, or release the stance, but it is quite the contrary. The driver calling for a "hang" instructs the team members to stand in place, drop their center of gravity, and hang tight using their weight as an anchor. Feet are planted into the ground and there is limited movement. This tactic is used to wear down the opposing team in their pull efforts by providing resistance. It is the idea of a relentless refusal to be moved by the fight in front of you. The combined weight and resilient effort in a "hang" state provides stabilization that makes it hard for the opponent to get the upper hand. The hang is the equivalent of being rooted, unshaken, or immovable despite the onset of attacks coming at you.

Contrarily, the driver can call for a "pull" in the game of tug of war which prompts the team members to dig in their heels and collectively power walk backwards without surrender. This is executed by a coordinated, all-out effort to dominate the opposing forces. When life hits hard, God calls for us to tighten our grip and pull with all of our might, resisting the urge to let go of our rope—hope. The good news is that we are not pulling alone. The Lord has sent us a host of angels to help tow the load and fight with us.

While *waiting*, there will be times when we must remain steadfast in our situation (hang) and times when we must pursue our destiny with full force while hauling the weight our adversary loads on us (pull). In either case, we can't do it alone, so our best option is to cling tightly to the directions of our Driver—God. He has the big picture in His view and will give us the command to secure the victory.

In your wait . . . release the weight of control. Allow God to direct you on when to strengthen your spirit in pursuit and when to rest in His promises.

Let's Weigh In

In what areas of your life are you hanging (steadfast/immovable)? In what areas of your life are you pulling (persevering/bearing through it)?

What are some immediate steps you can take to relinquish control in the areas listed above and completely rely on God's guidance?

<u>Scriptures</u>

I will instruct you and teach you in the way you should go; I will guide you with My eye (Psalm 32:8).

Your own ears will hear him. Right behind you a voice will say, "This is the way you should go," whether to the right or to the left (Isaiah 30:21).

<u>Prayer</u>

Heavenly Father, forgive me for all the times I have tried to carry life's load in my own strength. You are my Helper. Please order my steps and make clear the direction in which I should go. Teach me to know when to fortify myself for the battle and when to rest in Your sovereignty. In Jesus' Name.

Day Seven

Trust Fall

Every hot July summer of my teen years, I participated in our dance team intensives; a gruesome two-week camp that consisted of eight to ten hours of nonstop dancing each day. Any break that we could get from high kicking in the fields was heaven-sent, so when the coaches called a break for team building activities, we were all for it. One in particular that I remember most is Trust Fall.

Trust Fall is a game that many businesses, sports teams, and church organizations use to build trust amongst their members and teammates. One person crosses their arms over their chest, closes their eyes, and blindly falls back with the hope that the person behind them catches them before they hit the ground. *Whew!* Just thinking about that gives me anxiety. Why? Because one bad experience with Peggy and a bruised bum spurred my fear of playing this game. That's right, when yours truly finally stopped trembling and worked up the nerve to faithfully fall, good 'ole Peggy got distracted and my behind was introduced to the gym floor. Since then, my trust falls have been limited.

Can you relate? How about this; have you ever eaten at a particular fast-food restaurant and suffered food poisoning? What are the chances that you return to that restaurant? Slim to none if you are anything like me, for fear that it will happen again.

I believe this holds true in our daily lives. For many of us, the areas where we have been hurt or let down by others tend to be the areas where fear has settled in and planted its roots. We become demoralized at the thought of reliving a situation. From that moment on, hesitancy is incubated, and every step becomes a calculated move based upon the reasoning of our past experiences.

I know in the valley of my waiting season, the spirit of fear heavily kicked in after my miscarriage. The fear of having another miscarriage troubled my spirit. Not to mention, if the intense stomach pains of that incident were anything like labor pains, then I was petrified. Understandable fears giving my previous episode, but fear, nonetheless, that paralyzed me and created apprehension in my pursuit of a family.

Another fear that can stifle our *wait* is the worry that what we are believing God for, will never happen. Again, this stems from our experience or lack thereof. If we have yet to see our promise manifest, it becomes difficult to envision it coming into fruition. The longer our desires tarry, the deeper the fears embed into our minds, giving way to hesitancy, resistance, and even hopelessness.

The truth of the matter is, fear comes boxed in all types of bows of deception that can stem from one unfortunate or unfavorable situation. I would imagine that if I had a window view of your soul, I'd find some type of fear brewing in silence. Ever faced the fear of rejection? Fear of failure? Fear of disappointment? Fear of inadequacy? Fear of judgment? Fear of change? How about fear of the unknown? Pick one as any of them can deaden your procession into the promises of God.

God wants to untangle the fears that are choking your destiny. He wants you to lean back and to trust Him with your whole heart, and with each trust fall, you will gain more and more confidence in His security and faithfulness. You just have to trust Him enough to move forward in faith. Don't let what you see or don't see dictate what you know about God. Have faith that He will catch you. Remember, we are to walk by faith, not by sight (2 Corinthians 5:7). Take the plunge. Are you ready? Cross your arms, close your eyes, take a deep breath, and fall back into the arms of the Father. I guarantee He is a safe place to land. Trust Him.

In your _wait_ . . . release the weight of fear. Don't be moved by what you see or don't see. Trust God with your whole heart.

Let's Weigh In

What experience can you recall in your life that left you fearful of revisiting that experience?

What trust falls (fears) do you feel are paralyzing you from your destiny?

How can you take immediate steps to build your trust in God in those areas?

<u>Scriptures</u>

For God has not given us a spirit of fear, but of power and of love and of a sound mind (2 Timothy 1:7).

When I am afraid I will put my trust in you (Psalm 56:3).

For we were saved in this hope, but hope that is seen is not hope; for why does one hope for what he sees (Romans 8:24)?

<u>Prayer</u>

Spirit of the Living God, Your Word says that You have not given me a spirit of fear but of power, love, and a sound mind. Therefore, I bind up the fear of _____ and release Your love in place of it. Reveal any hidden fears that are lying dormant in my life so that I can surrender them to You. Lead me into a deeper place of trusting You with my whole heart. In Jesus' Name.

Day Eight

Quiet Game

Who can remember a time in school when students got rowdy and a teacher said, "Ok guys, let's play a game!" Excitedly the kids would settle down and prepare for some fun when the teacher continued with, "It's called … the quiet game." Moans and groans filled the room because we weren't naive to this ageless trick. More of a prank than a game but regardless, I deem it a pitiful attempt by parents and teachers to solicit a few moments of peace and quiet.

The rules of the game are simple—whoever remains silent the longest wins. No special technique or strategy, just a competition of stillness. I would be remiss if I didn't state that the prizes for this game never amounted to the efforts I put into holding my tongue. The mere idea of being quiet triggered an undeniable itch to speak. Repressing my impulse to talk was always met with challenges. Needless to say, this game was not my strong suit.

We live in a chaotic world and with all the busyness that consumes our life many of us can use a little peace and quiet now and again. But, at the same time, there is something about involuntary silence that makes us uncomfortable. We have gotten so accustomed to the necessity of noise that stillness becomes an awkward disposition. I believe this is why it is difficult for believers to sit still in the presence of God.

Personally, I have yet to master the art of stillness. I see this flaw in its most heightened state during my prayer time. I find myself bringing a laundry list of requests, demands, and complaints to God without waiting in his presence to see if He has anything to offer me in exchange. And even on the days that I embrace the stillness of meditation, in less than no time, the silence is eventually filled with extraneous activities like picking lint off the floor or refolding a disheveled blanket. Before I know it, quiet time has been infiltrated by a full-blown to-do-list lodged into my brain.

God wants our undivided attention. He constantly desires to communicate His will for our lives but our hectic lifestyles are thwarting the transmission line. Yes, the stillness, the quietness, might be uncomfortable but it is necessary. Jesus understood the importance of this sacred time with the Father. Jesus often withdrew to a quiet place to commune with the Father (Mark 1:35). If Jesus needed this intimate time with our Father, I presume we need it even more so.

I can admit, I am guilty of constantly filling up my silence with busyness especially during difficult seasons of *waiting*. I would much rather occupy my time with insignificant activities than feel the frustrations of delayed promises. In those periods of waiting, my quiet time with God can feel uncomfortable because it forces me to face my disappointments and choose to rely on God's presence for peace. Unlike a candy reward given by a teacher who deemed me the winner of the quiet game, the benefits of playing this game with God are insurmountable. In His presence, there is peace, joy, wisdom, strength, and strategy. We just have to sit there long enough to receive it.

In your wait . . . release the weight of *busyness*. Quiet yourself in the presence of God and give Him time to respond.

Let's Weigh In

How has a busy lifestyle impeded your quiet time with God?

What are some immediate steps you can take to ensure you carve out time for quiet stillness with God?

<u>Scriptures</u>

Let all that I am wait quietly before God, for my hope is in him (Psalm 62:5).

Be still, and know that I am God (Psalm 46:10).

Quiet down before God, be prayerful before him (Psalm 37:7 MSG).

<u>Prayer</u>

Lord, I commit to rearranging my schedule so that I don't forfeit my quiet time with You. Teach me how to prioritize my day, set boundaries on my time, and make You the center of my life. As I pray and meditate on Your Word, let my mind and heart be silent before You. Let Your peace calm the chaos that surrounds me daily. Let Your presence arrest me as I immerse myself in Your love. In Jesus' Name.

Day Nine

Twister

Right hand, yellow. Left foot, blue. Left hand, green. Right foot, red. It's Twister— "the game that ties you up in knots." Give the spinner a whirl and tap into your inner contortionism by putting your body parts on a vacant circle of the color called out by the referee. At first glance, this seems like a piece of cake. You plan moves in your head and hit the mat with confidence that you will be the last one standing until you find yourself wrapped up like a pretzel on the verge of toppling over. Twists and turns have you crouching over and barely able to maintain your balance. Wow! Doesn't that sound like the game of *life?*

We start off thinking we know how it's going to play out. *Graduate. Go to college. Get a job. Get married. Have kids. Become a Millionaire. Retire. I got this. Let's go!* Then we step on that mat (life), the wheel is spun, and before long, we are wrapped in the heartaches and hassles, caught in tangles of disappointment, and forced to balance trials that threaten to knock us over. Just me? Oh, I see a hand in the back row! Glad I am not alone.

The twists and turns we experience throughout life are usually nothing like what we've anticipated for ourselves. Unforeseen tragedy, unmet expectations, unfortunate losses, or undeserved heartbreaks can appear to steal our *happily ever after.*

And when life hits hard and our hope is dashed, the human tendency is to get discouraged. The confidence we had in our plans is shot and we are left in a precarious position wondering if the next spin will take us out. In the Bible, Hannah's story is a prime example of the weight of discouragement (1 Samuel 1).

Hannah experienced a downpour of discouragement that left her stressed out and empty on the inside. The plan she drafted for herself did not resemble that which was illustrated in her life. Unable to bear children, Hannah felt like a complete failure as a wife. During Old Testament times, infertility was considered a social embarrassment. In Middle Eastern culture, if barren, the wife would be subject to allowing a maidservant to marry her husband for the sake of childbearing. So not only was Hannah's deepest desires unfulfilled, but she also had to share her man with his second wife, Peninnah. Sounds like a recipe for discord and, in fact, it was. For years, Peninnah ridiculed and taunted Hannah by cruelly gloating in her own fertile womb.

Hannah's anguish grew so deep that it permeated her physical body inhibiting her ability to eat. But in the pits of her despair, instead of giving up hope, Hannah went to the one person that could heal her broken heart—God.

In verse 10, we find Hannah in the sanctuary weeping uncontrollably at the altar. So much so that the priest, Eli, took notice of her loud blubbering and assumed she was intoxicated. "Must you come here drunk?" he demanded. "Throw away your wine!" (v. 14 NLT). Hannah immediately elucidated "Oh no, sir!" she replied. "I haven't been drinking wine or anything stronger. But I am very discouraged, and I was pouring out my heart to the Lord. Don't think I am a wicked woman! For I have been praying out of great anguish and sorrow" (vs. 15–16 NLT). Hearing this, Eli comforted and encouraged her. "In that case," (he) said, "go in peace! May the God of Israel grant the request you have asked of Him" (v. 17 NLT).

It is difficult to walk away encouraged when you are staring at the knots of a tangled life, but in this passage, Hannah gives us the antidote to discouragement. First, pray. Be honest with God and tell Him how you really feel. He can handle it. Hannah brought her most authentic self before God—angry, bitter, resentful, broken, and defeated (v. 16). Second, release. After you pray about your problems, leave those anxieties with God. Hannah relinquished every burden that consumed her at the altar (v. 18). Finally, surround yourself with a small village of believers that can uplift you when you need it. Eli consoled Hannah and sent her off with a blessing, encouraging her to "go in peace"—leaving the weight of discouragement behind and receiving God's promises with gratitude and expectation (vs. 17–18).

Life is a test of balance, endurance, and flexibility, just like the game Twister. Be it discouragement because of singleness, barrenness, a failing marriage, or financial hardship, trust that God will help you overcome. When life twists you in every direction, garner strength from Hannah's story knowing the best is yet to come. I believe if Hannah could give us any advice—five children later—I am sure it would be, "You might encounter awkward twists and some uncomfortable turns in your journey, but at the end of the day, it is worth the wait."

In your wait…release the weight of discouragement. Trust God with your burdens. He is ready to receive them and renew your hope.

Let's Weigh In

Are there any challenges in your life that have you feeling discouraged and unsure about your future? If so, list them.

Are you willing to commit to releasing those dilemmas to God? If so, pray the prayer below and receive the peace of God.

Scriptures

Be strong and courageous. Do not be afraid; do not be discouraged, for the LORD your God will be with you wherever you go (Joshua 1:9 NIV).

May the God of hope fill you with all joy and peace as you trust in him, so that you may overflow with hope by the power of the Holy Spirit (Romans 15:13 NIV).

Prayer

Lord, I know my life will not always go as I have planned, but You have promised me peace in the midst of adversity. When my expectations are crushed and I am faced with discouragement or distress, revive my countenance. Send an encouraging word to restore my hope in You. Remove any seeds of darkness that have taken root as a result of disappointment and fill me with the joy of my salvation, which is in Christ Jesus. In Jesus' Name.

Day Ten

Monopoly

Have you ever tried to pay for groceries at your local market using Japanese Yen? Probably not—at least not in America where the currency is the U.S. Dollar. You would be denied and possibly booted out of the store. Why? Because every nation has a designated unit of currency that is used to acquire goods and services. Ironically, I learned this at a young age when trying to use Monopoly money to purchase candy from a convenience store.

Monopoly is the well-loved family game most parents used to school their kids on the value of money. At the start of the game, each player is endowed with the same amount of monopoly dollars to start their expedition. These dollars can be used in any transaction including buying a house, purchasing a lot, paying rent, making a trade, or getting out of jail. While the currency enables you to maneuver as desired, outside of the board game it has no value.

Back in the day, one of my first major gigs as a professional dancer was a tour overseas. I, along with a couple of my peers, were virgins to the international travel experience, but the artist's manager was a seasoned traveler. Because our schedule was tight, he stressed the importance of exchanging currency in advance to alleviate purchase dilemmas. I didn't take his expertise lightly and immediately exchanged my currency upon arrival while others did not take heed to the advice.

After leaving the airport, we stopped for lunch before heading to rehearsals. When it came time to pay for our meal, a fellow colleague (one who didn't listen) placed U.S. Dollars into the bill presenter. The waiter kindly addressed the matter via a translator and explained that they do not accept the U.S. Dollar.

"Are you serious? Everyone accepts the U.S. Dollar," my associate boldly stated.

"We only accept the Taiwanese Dollar here," replied the waiter.

Shocked by the waiter's sudden shift to our native language, we burst out laughing as our friend's ego was shattered. In ignorance, he assumed the U.S. Dollar was a universally accepted currency, but the only effective currency was the one recognized by that country.

The same goes for your life in the spirit realm where faith is the medium of exchange. It's the only currency that Heaven responds to. Pastor Michael Meyers summed this up when he said, "I have heard people angry at God because they got no response from Him; because of trying to move Jesus with their pain, their tears, their need, their hardship, their self-righteousness, their works, their sense of entitlement, etc."

Unfortunately, none of those natural factors move the hand of God. While He is sensitive to our feelings, He is not influenced by them. He is prompted by the currency of faith. It is similar to my friend trying to purchase a meal overseas with the U.S. dollar, or me trying to buy candy with make-believe money. In order for these transactions to be completed, the acceptable currency must be utilized.

Hebrews 11:6 tells us that "without faith it is impossible to please (God), for he who comes to God must believe that He is, and that He is a rewarder of those who diligently seek Him." God is waiting to answer our prayers even if our faith is as small as a mustard seed (Matthew 17:20). A little bit of faith can go a long way; it too has value and God is able to do mighty things with what you have.

Faith not only enables you to achieve the unimaginable, but it also overwhelms the doubts and fears in your heart when unforeseeable situations present themselves. That same faith also challenges you to step away from what you know to be true in the natural into the supernatural where nothing is impossible.

Have faith for your future spouse. Have faith for your children. Have faith for your career. Have faith for your healing. Have faith for your finances. Have faith—period.

Take this to the bank, when you have faith (your currency) with you throughout life (a trip around the Monopoly board), there is nothing that can stop you from winning.

In your *wait* . . . release the weight of the natural (what you know to be true) in exchange for the supernatural (what God says to be true). Release your faith; It is the only currency that gets God's attention.

Let's Weigh In

What currency are you currently using to try to get God's attention?

If faith is the currency of Heaven (supernatural), what are some ways you can fortify your faith in times of uncertainty?

<u>Scriptures</u>

Now faith is the substance of things hoped for, the evidence of things not seen (Hebrews 11:1).

Therefore, I say unto you, whatsoever things you desire, when you pray, believe that you receive them, and you shall have them (Mark 11:24).

<u>Prayer</u>

Jesus, I want to have audacious faith. I want to believe You for the impossible but sometimes I allow my doubts to overwhelm me. I know that fear and doubt are natural weights that challenge my faith muscles. Show me how to develop a life of constant faith and belief. Make me unflappable when fear and doubt rise up. Faith is a gift from You, and I want more of it. Increase my faith because faith leads the way to answered prayers. In Jesus' Name.

Day Eleven

Let's Make A Deal

One of my mom's favorite game shows is *Let's Make A Deal*—the Wayne Brady version because he is hilarious. It's a classic game where a contestant—dressed in the most extravagant costume—is granted something of value by the host (dealer) and is given the option to exchange it for a different item. The contestant—now known as the trader—usually has a tough time deciding because the new award is concealed behind a door. The unknown prize could be a fabulous gift like a car, a trip, or a decked-out game room. It can also be what is called a *zonk,* a prize of little or no worth to the trader.

You can find my mom yelling at the TV "Don't do it. Keep what you have," while watching the contestant debate on which to choose. The truth is, my mom doesn't know what's behind the door. She just wants the contestant to win; to be content with what they have and not risk it for something of no value to their life.

We too have the option of deciding which doors to choose when pedaling through life; the good news is most of our doors are marked by the Word of God which gives us insight on which ones to access.

Recently, while stuck in my waiting season, I found myself constantly being presented with two *trap* doors that proved worthless and detrimental to my destiny. I like to call them the *zonks* of life—envy and comparison. No doubt about it, entertaining either of these is a sure foot into a delayed destiny.

Many of us know these two *zonks* to be stifling entities, somehow, we still find ourselves looking at the next person wondering why our life doesn't look like theirs. Even the most *accomplished* person scrolls down their social media feed coveting certain aspects of someone else's life.

If we take a more extensive look, we'll find that a common crutch of envy and comparison is self-doubt—the lack of confidence in ourselves or our ability. I'll go even further and reveal that envy and comparison are also deeply rooted in our lack of *Godfidence*—the confidence we have in God or His ability.

The only way to conquer the battle of envy and comparison is to win the war of contentment. Therefore, while you wait for your promise, be at peace with the journey you are on. Be still. Don't fight your slow seasons—you know, the seasons that seem like God is not moving. Those are your stretching seasons. Enjoy them and take heed because God is teaching you patience and culminating you for what's in store.

I'll leave you with one of my go-to scriptures that I quote when envy or comparison rises up in my spirit. It's Proverbs 20:21: *"An inheritance claimed too soon will not be blessed in the end."*

Basically, this scripture underscores the importance of God's *perfect* timing. God wants us to win and that *win* can mean wait. God doesn't want to release anything before it's time. That can be disastrous! To make it practical for you, would you give the keys to your brand new car to a ten-year-old? *No Way!* You would never hand those keys to anyone that isn't mature enough to comprehend the value of that car.

God is your host in life's game of *Let's Make A Deal* and what He has given you is precious. Your life, your dreams, and your purpose are all invaluable and custom-made by Your Heavenly Father. That means recognizing and cherishing the gifts He has already blessed you with while you wait. So, *Let's Make A Deal*. Opt-out of envy and comparison, and choose to be content and grateful with what God has designed specifically for you. *No zonks!* You will win every time!

In your wait . . . release the weights of envy and comparison. Find contentment and joy in your personal journey. God makes no mistakes. You are right where you are supposed to be.

Let's Weigh In

Write down the areas where you see yourself envious or comparing your life to that of others.

What steps will you take to combat the feeling of envy? What are some ways that you can find contentment in your journey?

Scriptures

Let's just go ahead and be what we were made to be, without enviously or pridefully comparing ourselves with each other, or trying to be something we aren't (Romans 12:6 MSG).

I know what it is to be in need, and I know what it is to have plenty. I have learned the secret of being content in any and every situation, whether well fed or hungry, whether living in plenty or in want. I can do all this through him who gives me strength (Philippians 4:12-13).

Prayer

Father God, forgive me for not trusting You with my plans. When things don't work out the way that I desire or expect, help me to be content. I confess any envy and comparison that has left me in doubt that You will not come through on Your promises. When I am overcome with envy, comparison, and skepticism, give me confidence in Your ability to do the miraculous in my life. Remind me that I am uniquely made, with a special purpose ordained specifically for *me*. Replace these fears with the peace of God and the joy of contentment—for You started this work within me and I believe by faith that You will complete it. In Jesus' Name.

Day Twelve

Hide and Seek

". . . Ninety-eight, ninety-nine, one hundred. Ready or not here I come." That was the indicator for every player to expedite their plan and be securely tucked away in the best hiding place so that they are not found by "it" (the seeker). You know the game. Hide and Seek! The human scavenger hunt that every adolescent loved to play.

Most players opt to be the hider rather than the seeker. Why? Being the seeker takes work. The seeker is on a constant quest to find hiders that might not be in plain sight. I remember playing with my friends when I was younger and I could find some of them expeditiously because they hid in obvious places. However, others took the game more seriously and hid so well it was borderline impossible to locate them.

Does it ever appear to you that God is playing a game of Hide and Seek? When you are faced with insurmountable disappointments and begging God for clarity, does it feel like He has found the best hiding place ever? I don't know about you, but there have been times during my waiting season when God's presence appeared to be nowhere in sight. It felt like He was playing a *Divine* game of *Hide and Seek* if you will, and the more angst I was about a situation the harder it was to find Him. *Is God here? Does He care?*

With minimum words of confirmation, we can easily misconstrue God's silence for absence. The truth is, God longs to be sought out. He says, "When you come looking for me, you will find me. Yes when you get serious about finding me and want it more than anything else, I'll make sure you won't be disappointed" (Jeremiah 29:13 MSG). In other words, it is in our wholehearted pursuit that God reveals Himself. Sometimes it's as easy to find God as seeing a hider's feet sticking out from behind the curtain. Other times it takes a while to find God, not because He doesn't want to be found, but He wants us to dig deeper. If we put forth minimal effort in seeking His *will,* then we can't expect God to take us seriously. God delights in concealing things just to get us to draw near and diligently seek Him (Proverbs 25:2).

Do you recall those times when you stumbled upon the best hiding places while playing Hide and Seek? I know that if I presumed too much time had passed and the seeker hadn't a clue of where I was then I would make a subtle noise or giggle to hint to the seeker that they were close. If the seeker was lucky, sure enough, the seeker would spot me and the chase to home base would begin.

Essentially, every hider in the game wants to be found. It is the very essence of the game. God wants to be found; and just like that snicker or giggle in the game of Hide and Seek that exposes a hider's whereabouts to the seeker, God always makes Himself known.

When you don't hear Him, when you don't see Him, when you can't feel Him, perhaps it is time to jump in a game of *Hide and Seek* with the Master watching and waiting for those moments when He makes Himself known.

In your wait...release the weight of uncertainty. Seek God with all your heart. He will make Himself known.

Let's Weigh In

List areas of your life where you are uncertain of God's plan for you.

What are ways you can diligently seek God in those areas during your *waiting* season?

Scriptures

But from there you will seek the Lord your God, and you will find Him if you seek Him with all your heart and with all your soul (Deuteronomy 4:29).

Ask, and it will be given to you; seek, and you will find; knock, and it will be opened to you (Matthew 7:7).

Prayer

Father God, when I can't find You, remind me of Your steadfast and immovable spirit. When I am faced with the uncertainty of Your presence, show me that You are near. Your Word says that when I draw near to You, You will draw near to me. Therefore, I commit to seeking You with my whole heart. I will consistently ask You for Your guidance. I will diligently seek Your ways. I will persistently knock on Your door until You answer with Your plans or Your presence. God, I make You my quest and I will pursue You today, and every day of my life. In Jesus' Name.

Day Thirteen

Madden

With over 100 million copies sold, there is no doubt that *Madden NFL* is one of the best-selling sports video games to date. My brothers and I used to rent this game from Blockbuster Video Store in a shameless attempt to teach me about football. I thank Professor John Madden for his masterpiece that assisted in schooling me on the game. I am proud to say *I am a girl who loves football*. As the catchphrase goes, "Girls who love football aren't weird. They are a rare gift from God and deserve bigger diamonds."

Football is the most popular sport in America. For those that are not as savvy with the sport, the goal is the same as any other sport: score more points than the other team. However, I don't believe there is another game that requires as much strategy and execution to do so. In most cases, the job of the offense is to score points and wear down the defense in the process. The defense, on the other hand, is about defending their territory and prohibiting the other team from scoring points. The best teams are those that are able to execute on offense and defense. Similar to the game of football, the only way to succeed in life is to ensure that you are playing both offense and defense.

Offense

When on offense, you are in control of the ball. Your objective is to be proactive and aggressive because your opponent's mission is to stop you from progressing forward. But this is where the playbook is of the utmost importance. In it lie the strategies and tactics necessary to pulverize your opposition.

Our playbook for life is The Word of God, the Bible. Satan is our opponent, and his sole purpose is to stop us from *receiving* the promises of God. The Bible is loaded with play calls such as prayer, meditation on His word, worship, and obedience; all of which are imperative to reach our goal post. Simply put, it's the *Master's* game plan. Without it, we would be in a state of utter confusion, but with it, we have the ability to attack anything that comes up against us.

In the very first chapter of Psalms, the Word tells us to delight ourselves in The Law of the Lord (the playbook) and to meditate on scripture day and night (Psalm 1:1–2). In order to triumph over life's adversaries, we must master and execute the playbook by reading, studying, and applying it to our life. When God's playbook is second nature to us, then our reserve tank is stored up for a rainy day. So, when Satan throws a ruse and we see the enemy lining up to thwart our play (test our faith), we have enough in us to change up the play call and still progress forward.

On offense, you don't wait for the enemy to attack (to grab your playbook); no, you are in relentless pursuit, constantly chewing on the Word of God, and never losing sight of His promises. When you know the playbook (the Word of God), you are less susceptible to the enemy's surprise attacks. Every time you fight the enemy with the Word, you gain yardage. Follow the plays given and you are destined to get points on the board, thus, keeping your opponent at bay.

Defense

Your defensive strategy has to be just as strong if not stronger than your offensive strategy. On defense, you must protect yourself from the tricks of the enemy (deception) and sinful nature. If the enemy takes ground and continues to gain yardage in your life, then he wins because you never move forward. Don't allow him to set foot on your side of the field and the way to do that is by staying rooted in the Word of God, which is the leverage you need to keep from being moved by the enemy's attacks.

Play-Action is when the quarterback fakes a run and throws a pass. For lack of better words, deception. As the father of lies,

Satan wants you to believe that you are not good enough to win the game; and you are not worthy of God's promises.

Satan is the mastermind of deception, always hiding his real intentions, and the lies he presents to you can cause you to spiral into a world of unbelief.

The enemy's advances consisted of telling me that God didn't care about me. I would never be successful. I would never have kids. I would die before my time. And that my past mistakes disqualified me from God's promises—along with a host of other falsities.

But in fact, God's Word says the complete opposite. The Bible says I am the apple of His eye (Psalm 17:8). God says I will be fruitful and multiply (Genesis 9:7). God says I will have a long life and be successful (Psalm 91:16, Proverbs 3:4 ESV). God says I am forgiven of my past (Hebrews 10:17). And God says that all things work together for my good and His glory (Romans 8:28).

Believe it or not, that's only a smidgen of over five thousand promises in the Bible so don't believe the hype of the enemy. Satan wants to destroy your faith.

Every lie the enemy can dredge up from the pits of hell in order to take your focus off of the game, he will. Chances are he has already tried to deceive you into thinking things about yourself that are contrary to what God says about you.

Game Time

In truth and transparency, we have all fallen for the okey-doke of the enemy. But the game is not over. We might feel like we are in the 4th quarter with only two minutes left in the game and the enemy has the upper hand. But rest assured a victory is in store for us.

Satan only has the power *we* give him, but he's still not as powerful as our God! Therefore, let's gear up with the whole armor of God (Ephesians 6:11), grab our *Playbook*, and let the ultimate Coach (our Lord, and Savior) usher us into a win of a lifetime. GAME ON!

In your wait…release the weight of deception. Deception is a distraction from your ultimate goal. God's Word is your playbook to ensure victory over all the plans of the enemy.

Let's Weigh In

What are some lies Satan tries to get you to believe about yourself?

What steps can you take to get more acquainted with your Playbook (Bible)?

<u>Scriptures</u>

Study this Book of Instruction continually. Meditate on it day and night so you will be sure to obey everything written in it. Only then will you prosper and succeed in all you do (Joshua 1:8 NLT).

Stay alert! Watch out for your great enemy, the devil. He prowls around like a roaring lion, looking for someone to devour (1 Peter 5:8 NLT).

Put on the full armor that God gives, so you can defend yourself against the devil's tricks (Ephesians 6:11).

Prayer

Heavenly Father, as I study Your Word, embed the scriptures deep into my heart so that my arsenal is full and I am always ready for battle. I am fully aware that I have an adversary that is out to steal, kill, and destroy my purpose. Let Your Word be a lamp unto my feet and a light unto my path that exposes Satan's schemes that are designed to dismantle my faith. I refuse to be deceived by his lies and counter every attack of the enemy with Your Word. And if this war gets too big to fight, I know that You will fight my battle for me, Oh Lord, my *Great Defender.* No weapon formed against me shall prosper. In Jesus' Name.

Day Fourteen

Connect 4

Connect 4 is the classic two-player strategy game also known as *Four in a Row.* The objective is pretty evident from the title. Each player takes turns dropping their specified red or black chips into a column. The first player to align their four chips in a row wins. The strategy seems simple—*play the right moves*—but in fact, *Connect 4* requires fast thinking and a fair amount of foresight.

Life, by its very nature, also requires a plan of action and a bit of perspicacity. Since we are not immune to the problems of life, I deem it necessary to put into practice some key components when you feel stuck in the *waiting* room of life. Worrying won't add one single moment to your life (Luke 12: 25), but *connecting* these four power essentials: Prayer, Praise, Perspective, and Perseverance, will help with keeping you afloat when rocked by the storms of life.

Connection #1: The Power of Prayer

I consider prayer, the oxygen to my soul, the fuel to my tank, the super to my natural. It's the non-negotiable time that I spend communing with God. It's a conversation, a two-way street that consists of not only speaking but also listening.

Prayer is not running down a laundry list of requests and leaving. God is not a genie in a bottle. Ever heard the saying "listen twice as much as you speak"? Well, the same principle applies here. Prayer is about adoration, meditation, and supplication—it's the cultivation of a deep-rooted connection with our Creator.

Prayer is the key that unlocks the mysteries of God and brings you into a deeper understanding of not only His character but also His will for your life. When walking under the weight of unanswered prayers, connecting with the Father might be the last thing you feel like doing, but it is vital to your winning strategy. In times of overwhelming situations, instead of abandoning God, we must draw closer to Him by reading and praying His Word.

History has shown that prayer is *powerful* and has the ability to turn situations around. One of my favorite stories in the Bible that demonstrates this well is located in 2 Kings 20 when King Hezekiah became terminally ill and was told by the prophet Isaiah to prepare for death. "(Hezekiah) turned his face toward the wall, and prayed to the Lord" (v. 2). The Lord changed his mind and said, "I have heard your prayer, I have seen your tears; surely I will heal you" (v. 5). And God added *fifteen* years to his life span.

Countless times in the Bible we see God manifesting His supernatural goodness as a result of prayer. Isaac "prayed to the Lord on behalf of his wife, because she was childless. The Lord answered his prayer, and his wife Rebekah became pregnant" (Genesis 25:21 NIV). Jonah, who was swallowed by a fish, "prayed to the Lord from the fish's belly" (Jonah 2:1). "Then the Lord ordered the fish to spit Jonah out onto the beach" (Jonah 2:10). Jehoshaphat received the intelligence that the Moabites and Ammonites were preparing to attack him and called for a nationwide prayer imploring God to intervene on their behalf and He delivered them from their enemies (2 Chronicles 20).

The prophet Elijah performed many miracles, signs, and wonders through prayer; one notable prayer was for the healing of a young boy. "Three times (Elijah) stretched himself out full-length on the boy, praying with all his might, 'God, my God, put breath back into this boy's body!' God listened to Elijah's prayer and put breath back into his body—he was alive!" (1 Kings 17:21–22). These are only a select few of the stories that embody God's wondrous works through *prayer.*

God admonishes us to "pray without ceasing" (1 Thessalonians 5:17), to "devote (ourselves) to prayer" (Colossians 4:2 NIV), and "pray about everything" (Philippians 4:6 NLT). Prayer is eminent to our lives and it moves God to action.

Prayer is a lifestyle. Walk in it!

Connection #2: The Power of Praise

When you struggle with the weight of a waiting season, one of the first things the enemy will do is attack your desire to worship. Satan understands that if he can silence you, he has a better chance of distorting your view of God—making you feel as if He isn't a Good Father. But, you see, praise is your secret protection against discouragement and defeat—*you can't worship and worry at the same time*. Praise helps redirect our thoughts back to God and His ability (or character) instead of our situation. A key ingredient that stokes our praise is recollection.

In Lamentations 3, Jeremiah depicts a candid canvas of his frustrations and blames God for his misfortunes: "(God) has besieged me and surrounded me with anguish and distress" (v. 5). "He has blocked my way with a high stone wall; He has made my road crooked" (v. 9). "He has dragged me off the path and torn me in pieces, leaving me helpless and devastated" (v. 11).

We can surmise from his etched words that Jeremiah was twinged with a heavy dose of *grief.* Evidently, the prophetic path God had called him to wasn't as easy as he imagined. This left him feeling desolate and defeated. As we continue reading Lamentations 3, we notice—right smack dab in the middle of the passage—Jeremiah flips the switch from deep agony to one of faith. He declared, "I have hope" (v. 21).

What would cause Jeremiah to suddenly start marching to the beat of a different drum? The answer—Recalling! Jeremiah's hope was restored when he reflected on the goodness of God. "Yet I still dare to hope when I remember this: The faithful love of the Lord never ends! His mercies never cease. Great is His faithfulness" (vs. 21–23 NLT). I don't know about you, but when I recall God's goodness, I can't help but praise Him.

Remembering God's love and mercy will incline you to praise Him daily. Psalm 34:1 says, "I will praise the Lord at all times; His praise shall continually be in my mouth." Your praise is a decree—a declaration. It is you putting a down payment on what you are believing. Worshipping while you wait tells God that you trust Him.

Having said that, when life's shadows distort your reality and clouds your vision, recollect the things the Lord has done for you and *praise* Him. It will sustain you and build your confidence that if He came through before, He will come through again. His record is perfect.

Praise is protection. Use it!

Connection #3: The Power of Perspective

The way people perceive trials often has a greater impact than the trial itself. How a situation is viewed determines the way a person feels about the situation. For example, one person may look at a job loss as a dire circumstance with concerns of financial struggles; another person may look at a job loss as an opportunity to start the business of their dreams. While one perceives it as a weight of uncertainty, the other eyes a suitable time to seize their destiny and emerge stronger than ever. Same scenario, two different perspectives.

Our day-to-day experiences help to shape our perspective on life and we define what makes sense to us through our *perspective*. Because our scope of life is limited to our reality, we tend to see only the current conditions when turmoil arises, while God sees the big picture (the eternal). Our goal is to seek God's perspective on our situations instead of relying on our own.

When traveling back home from the west coast one evening, our flight experienced some inclement weather that caused our pilots to reroute for landing. As I stared at the lightning through the window, my anxieties grew with the turbulence as we circled the dark skies. The only forewarning we received from the pilot was to ensure our seatbelts were fastened which did not ease my angst at all. While I presumed danger was ahead and a safe landing was sketchy, the pilot was cool, calm, and collected. Why? Because he had inside information.

The pilot received specific instructions from air traffic control on how to navigate through the storm. Although the pilot and I saw the same storm through the window he had insight from a greater perspective—air traffic control. This gave the pilot all the confidence he needed to safely and successfully land the plane. So, while I was terrified, the pilot was unbothered.

Because we aren't able to see life from a bird's eye view, we must rely on God to give us His perspective on problems so that we can see the big picture. If you take your eyes off God and look at your problem, you begin to lose perspective, which can cause you to lose faith.

We see this notion of perspective in 1 Samuel 17 when the Israelite army faced off against the Philistines. When challenged by Goliath, King Saul and the Israelites "were dismayed and greatly afraid" (v. 11). In their sight, they didn't stand a chance against a *giant* warrior like Goliath, but David saw the *giant* Goliath as a frail human summoned to his fate for defying Almighty God (v. 26). David kept his eyes on the Master, not the mountain.

The discomfort of life's difficulties may cause you to want to focus on your problem during your waiting season. Instead, focus on adopting God's perspective while you wait. It will transform how you view negative circumstances. I'll end with this tale in hopes that we all take a page out of Sam and Jed's book.

A Texas organization offered a bounty of $5000 for captured wolves. Two hunters named Sam and Jed decided to make some money catching wolves. Day and night they scoured the mountains and forests searching for their valuable prey. Exhausted after several days of hunting with no luck, *they both fell asleep. During the night, Sam suddenly woke up to find that he and Jed were surrounded by a pack of seventy wolves. With flaming red eyes, bared teeth, and low growls grumbling, the wolves snarled at the two hunters. Sam slowly reached over and nudged Jed and said, "Hey, wake up! We're rich!"*

Perspective! Many of us would have looked at this dilemma and thought, "It's a wrap … we're dead." But Sam didn't see those wolves as a threat but as an opening for abundance and increase. Change your *perspective* while you wait.

Perspective is a mindset. Shift it!

Connection #4: The Power of Perseverance

The final element I want to connect here is Perseverance. When you hear the word perseverance, what do you think of? For me, endurance comes to mind, in relation to running. However, I found that the word *endurance* is often tethered to physical strength—stamina, agility—whereas perseverance is the ability to *persist* in something despite facing adversity, difficulty, or a delay in achieved success.

God uses life's difficulties and the enemy's attacks to build our endurance and shape our character. Trials serve as sifters that differentiate believers from unbelievers. The Message version of the Bible puts it plainly, "Pure gold put in the fire comes out of it *proved* pure; genuine faith put through this suffering comes out *proved* genuine" (1 Peter 1:7 MSG).

There will always be pressures that foster discouragement during waiting periods and many, if not all of us, will experience challenging times. But our ability to persevere is tested through trials. "Suffering produces perseverance" (Romans 5:3 NIV) but we never persevere without the promise of a prize. Because Christ lives in us, we have the endurance we need to prevail in His strength. We have to choose to stay steadfast and hold firm to our faith when our faith is tested and opposed by adverse conditions. Perhaps the experience I had will help to paint a better picture of what I mean.

It was a beautiful summer day, so I decided to go to a nearby track for a run. I turned on the Nike Run Club app on my phone, strapped my phone to my arm, put my earbuds in, turned on my 5K playlist, and hit the pavement. Once I settled into the run, I heard the app announce that I was averaging an eleven-minute mile. On a good day, I was able to obtain a nine-minute mile, but the atmospheric conditions—100-degree weather—was not positively contributing to my pace.

Everything in me wanted to quit. I reduced my jog to a very fast walk as the combination of disappointment, discouragement, and *heat* exasperated me. But when an older lady lapped me, I was *done*! "That's it! I might as well quit," I groaned to myself. All I could think about was soothing my displeasure with a good old-fashion donut. I gradually transitioned to a walk (to my car) when I heard the voice on the app say, "Don't quit! You're almost there."

Her words leaped into my spirit and invigorated my aching bones and what was fatigue and exhaustion was immediately converted to energy.

"Why quit now?" I thought. Shortly after, adrenaline kicked in and I clocked my last mile in nine minutes.

My body was used to running 5Ks; training had produced that type of physical dexterity—endurance. But it took mental and physical willpower and determination to push past the heaviness and fight through. *Perseverance* is what propelled me to finish.

Waiting is tiring, but we persevere by moving ahead despite impediments and delays. Yes, it's difficult and it might appear that everyone is getting to the finish line before you, but we are to "run with perseverance the race marked out for *us*, fixing our eyes on Jesus, the pioneer and perfecter of faith" (Hebrews 12:1–2 NIV).

This isn't about beating the people running alongside you. It's about defeating the voices in your own head that cause you to want to give up on God. It's about resisting the urge to concede when the circumstances are not conducive to the desired journey. Don't give up. Push-through.

Perseverance is a muscle. Build it!

Connect 4: Prayer. Praise. Perspective. Perseverance. Got it?

In your wait ... release any and all **WEIGHTS** that are hindering you from believing God. Your game-winning strategy requires **Prayer, Praise, Perspective, and Perseverance.** Connect these 4 essential principles and you are sure to succeed in *The Game of Life.*

Let's Weigh In

What do you feel are the benefits of connecting with God through prayer?

What does it look like to praise and worship while you wait? How can you make praise a daily habit?

Compared to Sam and Jed, how would you have perceived the wolves' scenario? Do you often see challenges as advantageous or disadvantageous?

Why is perseverance important in life's journey? How do you overcome when your perseverance is tested?

<u>Scriptures</u>

Rejoice always, pray without ceasing, in everything give thanks; for this is the will of God in Christ Jesus for you (1 Thessalonians 5:16–18).

And do not be conformed to this world, but be transformed by the renewing of your mind, that you may prove what *is* that good and acceptable and perfect will of God (Romans 12:2).

And not only that, but we also glory in tribulations, knowing that tribulation produces perseverance; and perseverance, character; and character, hope (Romans 5:3–4).

Prayer

My Gracious God, I enter into this prayer with praise and thanksgiving for Your loving kindness and gentle mercies. You are majestic in all of Your ways and it is an honor to bring my requests before You this day. Thank You for hearing my prayers and guiding me with Your wisdom. Renew my mind, Father, so that I can see things from Your perspective. I know that tribulations produce perseverance so help me fight the good fight of faith. And when the road gets difficult and my knees get weak, strengthen me for the journey ahead. Hold me steady with Your righteous right hand so that I can finish the race You have set before me. I praise You in advance for the wonderful victories ahead. In Jesus' Name.

Acknowledgments

Before I thank anyone, I have to thank God. For years, I wallowed in self-pity not understanding why this was the chosen path for me, but now … I know. Thank you, Lord. You are the pen of a ready writer—We did it! #forsuchatimeasthis

Walter, thank you for being my safe *haven*, helpmate, soundboard, voice-of-reason, and best friend. I appreciate your vulnerability and strength during our waiting season. Thank you for allowing me to share our story. I love you!

This book would not be if there were no Eboni. That rhymed. Eboni Obanero, girl, that first draft was rough! But you said I was on to something and to keep pushing. Your friendship is immeasurable. I don't know what I'd do without you. Thank you for the countless days and nights of pounding this out with me. I owe you big time (unlimited babysitting on me).

Mama, thank you for always making yourself available to read my writing and offering feedback and suggestions to make it better. I'd be here for days on end expressing my gratitude for you and all you have done for me, so I'll spare the people the sentiments and wrap it up with I love you to the moon and back.

Thank you to the matriarch and wise one, Grannie James! I know for a fact that it's your daily 5 a.m. prayer calls with Aunt Margie that keeps me covered. I am beyond grateful that God has allowed you to see this milestone, and pray He graces you to see many more. If y'all need to find a scripture and don't have a Bible on hand, call Grannie James. She's got that Word tucked, locked, and loaded. Love you!

Dana Ellington, the best book strategist to walk God's green earth. Thank you for the wisdom, idea bouncing, and for graciously restructuring the lifelines (also known as deadlines) that I seemed to always miss.

Jamal Story, thank you for being my human dictionary and thesaurus. You are quite the wordsmith, my friend. You have a heart of pure gold and the mind of a genius. I appreciate your thought-provoking edits and challenging me to dig deep. Love you brother.

Kim Nolte, thank you for helping me whittle down the content and lock in the nuggets. You made the editing process fun and stress-free (sometimes). LOL!

Louis Cuthbert, better known as A King With A Camera. Thank you for a bomb photoshoot and cover design. You are always a blast to work with, but most importantly your vision is one straight from the Heavens. Keep doing God's work brother, you are killing it.

To my Dads. Biological - there would be no me without you. Literally! Loving the journey that we are on and looking forward to continuing to grow our relationship. Also, I must shout out my Bonus Dad, Darryl, for the constant love and support throughout my life.

To all of my family, friends, day ones, and ride-or-dies. I can't say thank you enough. My heart is full with all of the love and support. Grateful!

Diana, the ultimate prayer warrior that I am honored to call my friend. I do believe your intercession came through for your girl. You have been one of my biggest cheerleaders during this project and for that, I am immensely grateful.

Desiree, Yvette, Marquita, Bresha, Angel, Regine. You ladies are beyond amazing and your talents are unmatched. I hope I inspire you as much as you inspire me. Thank you for the part you played during this home stretch—accountability, offering concepts and strategies, reading my manuscript, sending encouraging words, listening to my rants, being an awesome gym buddy (not judging me when I broke down in the middle of our workouts), and of course, the random check-ins (that weren't so random, rather right on time).

To me, myself, and I—You go girl! You thought you weren't good enough, but you are. You thought you'd never finish, but you did.

Last, but certainly not least, to my Warriors. I am because of you. Thank you to my tribe – *Women Wives Warriors.* Thank you for attending every event, buying books, reading blogs, inviting me to teach and speak, listening to podcasts, liking posts, and sharing my silly content with others. You inspire me to keep inspiring you. We make *purpose* look good, ladies. Let's keep being D.O.P. (Different On Purpose).

Notes/References

1. Gabrielle Union Interview

   https://www.redbookmag.com/beauty/anti-aging/a39713/redbook-october-ageless-issue/

2. Tyra Banks-The Fab Life Show (transcribed)

   https://www.youtube.com/watch?v=qoCO06M1Mzs&feature=emb_title

3. The World Health Organization

   https://www.who.int/reproductivehealth/topics/rtis/en/

4. The Very Well Family

   https://www.verywellfamily.com/does-an-hsg-hurt-1960165

5. Barna Group - ⅔ Christians

   https://www.barna.com/research/two-thirds-christians-face-doubt/

6. Barna Group - Spiritual Doubt

   https://www.barna.com/research/two-thirds-christians-face-doubt/

7. American Pregnancy Association

   https://americanpregnancy.org/getting-pregnant/hcg-levels/

8. American Pregnancy Association

   https://americanpregnancy.org/pregnancy-complications/d-and-c-procedure-after-miscarriage/

About the Author
Dacia James Lewis

Dacia James Lewis is wife to Walter and aunt/God-mother to several mentees and children. A multi-hyphenate with a passion for creating quality entertainment, Dacia is not only an accomplished choreographer, but she is also a director, producer, and business owner. She is the President of Women Wives Warriors and the owner of D.O.P. Entertainment. When she is not on television and film sets shooting with the stars, she enjoys creating content for her company and serving in youth ministries.

Dacia teaches master classes and speaks worldwide at dance studios, universities, conferences, and various church events. To those that know her best, Dacia is a lover of Jesus Christ, a ride-or-die friend that gives it straight—no chaser, and a giver of everything she has ... except her french fries.

If you enjoyed The Game of Life, avail yourself with additional resources or join our community at www.womenwiveswarriors.com. Subscribe to our email list for special bonus products/material.

Connect with Dacia on the following platforms. See her comical social media content and future engagements on the sites below.

Website: www.daciajames.com

Blog: www.womenwiveswarriors.com

Instagram: @daciajames/@womenwiveswarriors

Facebook: www.facebook.com/daciajames

Facebook Group: www.facebook.com/womenwiveswarriors